Courage of Innocence

A Saga of Italian Immigrants in the American Frontier

Ann Federici-Martin

authorHOUSE®

AuthorHouse™
1663 Liberty Drive, Suite 200
Bloomington, IN 47403
www.authorhouse.com
Phone: 1-800-839-8640

First published by AuthorHouse 2/9/2009

ISBN: 978-1-4389-2314-7 (sc)
ISBN: 978-1-4389-2315-4 (hc)

Printed in the United States of America
Bloomington, Indiana

This book is printed on acid-free paper.

Front cover image: A formal portrait of the Federici family taken in Denver in 1931 on the occasion of Fred's graduation from Denver University Law School. From left to right: the author, her brother Fred and sister Emma, Narciso, Divina, and brother Bill.

Spine image: Ann Federici-Martin in about 1924-1925

A favorite portrait of Ann's father, Narciso, fishing at Eagle Nest Lake, New Mexico. The hand-tinted photo resided on the buffet in the dining room of the "G and G House" in Cimarron for decades.

*This book is dedicated to my father, Narciso Federici;
a builder and a philosopher.*

As a young man he learned to work stone at the marble quarries of Massa Carrara, Italy, and as a mason on the Aswan Dam across the Nile River in Egypt. The money he saved from that job, and the skills he learned, allowed him to follow his dream to America where, with his wife, Divina, he courageously chiseled out a new life in New Mexico. There, he built stores, homes, a family, and, yes, an opera house.

Acknowledgements

To name all of the people who have inspired me and contributed to my being where I now am, as a person, a woman, an artist, and an author, would be a book in and of itself. First of all I want to acknowledge my family. It was the dreams and courage of my parents, Narciso and Divina Federici, that made it all come true. Because of them, we are Americans, we are New Mexicans, we are La Familia.

No less important are the roles that my brothers and sisters, Federico, Emmacita, Guliermo, and Benecia, played in my life. This is their story. A story that leads in an unbroken line to those of their children, their children's children, and their children's children's children, who continue to play out the roles that were handed them here in western America, and elsewhere in the world.

My husband, Curtis Martin, was the key to so many doors that opened to the person that I am now. He led me to big cities and foreign countries, to the halls of academia and the smoky rooms where the future of American politics was being forged, up countless streams and rivers to peaceful lakes and mountaintops. Through Curtis I met great politicians, world leaders, teachers, writers, scientists and philosophers. Not to mention a number of distinguished trout fishermen. It was Curtis who taught me to write; first and foremost through the exercise of reviewing and editing his countless manuscripts, short stories, and the galley proofs of his novel *The Hills of Home*.

To my sons, Brooke and Curt, and their wives Lucy and Marsha, and my grandchildren, Dylan and Hilary; you know that you are the people of which my dreams are made. Thank you for your faith in this project; I couldn't have done it without you. A particular thanks to Curt, who acted as my editor and publishing aide, and to Marsha for all of her work on the typing, cover design and layout.

Lastly, I want to thank Mrs. Pochel, my teacher in that little, one-room schoolhouse in the wilds of New Mexico who handed me my very first book. When I opened the cover of that book, I opened the world.

Thank you.

Ann Federici-Martin, Santa Fe, New Mexico. 2008.

Contents

From Apache Hill to Boulder

My story is inextricably woven into the stories of who my parents were, where they came from, what they envisioned for their children, and what they endured to pursue those dreams. The earliest things that I remember about myself and my family occurred at our ranch in Apache Hill, New Mexico. The stories of those eight years provide a unique and meaningful chronicle of an immigrant family that had come to America seeking a new and better life. Now, when I take the time to reflect on those years, I am engulfed with an appreciation of the amount of courage, strength, and patience that it must have taken for my parents to accomplish what they did.

My parents, Narciso and Divina, came from a meager little hilltop in northern Italy with a fantastic history of invaders that goes back to the Etruscans—the Etruscans being an obscure culture with, as yet, un-deciphered writings. Only the remains of their architecture, pottery, and the wall art of their stone "cities of the dead" gives us some clues.

My parents had never spoken to me about the Etruscans until I found out something about this fascinating culture by reading D.H. Lawrence's Etruscan Places. It was then that I realized my people, my forebears, were living on Etruscan soil among the hills that contained their relics and archaeology. When I mentioned this fact to my mother, she would think back to the Old Country and say, "Oh yes, I remember some of the old people talking about the ancient ones." She would remember the distant, round-topped hills near her home that were covered with chestnut trees and scrub oak and say "those were where the Etruscans lived. If you were to dig underneath those mounds you will find the burials and the terra cotta figures and art on the walls." However, my parents were always too busy to look into them. Besides, they were dead and past and they needed to think of the living and how to provide for themselves and the others of their village.

The Etruscan hills are across the world from Apache Hill, and the histories and cultures of both regions are centuries apart, but I think it is important for me to touch upon this because without this background you can never really know me, or understand what happened to me, or truly understand what it means for me to be a citizen of America in a modern university town surrounded by highly educated people in the fields of science and literature.

My early recollection of Apache Hill was the one-room house made of wood and tar-paper. At one end there was the coal and wood range surrounded by a few open, crudely built wooden shelves, a small wooden table, and four chairs. A large crock which held water was near the stove. The water was brought in by buckets from a spring that came out of the hillside near the cabin. The rest of the home consisted of a sheet stretched across a heavy wire which divided the room into two sections. There were no windows or doors in the sleeping area. The beds were platforms of wood upon which were mattresses made of striped blue and white ticking filled with bean shucks from the previous year's pinto bean crop.

As a child, I was very happy there. I had everything I needed. I had two active brothers, one older, and the other two years younger. I had parents who loved me and saw to it that I had plenty of good food and warmth. I had no toys or books, and certainly no radio or TV, but I had a pet chicken that followed me everywhere and even slept with me. My mother had taught me how to put a make-shift diaper on my hen, so we had no problems in that area.

My primary duty to the household was to keep the crock near the stove filled with water at all times. Since that supply of water took care of all washing, as well as human consumption needs, I was kept very busy running up and down that hill carrying a ten pound lard bucket full of water to keep the supply on tap. I even acquired a new name, "Little Miss Running Water."

We saw many coyotes and listened to their barks and howls at night. The rattlesnakes were also numerous and we were taught not to sit or walk anywhere without first checking the terrain carefully. A small rattlesnake shared the spring with me and I always looked forward to seeing him. I let him have first go at the water on those hot afternoons. Many years later I read a poem written by D.H. Lawrence entitled, "The Snake" and the emotions and feelings it evoked in me were very meaningful.

No one told me about the American Indians that had once lived there, but my curious eyes and hands found many of their special treasures. There was a reason for all these spear points and arrowheads. I found out later that the cut on the rim rock of the mountain at Apache Hill was part of the northern route of the Santa Fe Trail. The army, as well as the pioneers who took the trail over the mountain, probably found out the hard way how difficult it was to try to get to Santa Fe and California on this northern route, not only because of the rugged terrain, but also because of the constant threat of encounters with the natives.

The Opera House in the small historic village of Cimarron, New Mexico also played an important part in my growing up. It was here that I moved with my family after we left Apache Hill. Cimarron is a Spanish word that means "untamed" or "lawless" and my father thought that he might be able to change part of that image of the little isolated town. Coming from Italy, he had brought with him two important aspects that had shaped his life at an early age. One was his love for Italian opera and the other was the trade he had learned in the hills of Massa Carrara near a town named Prota. He was a stone cutter and stone mason. When my parents decided to settle in Cimarron, where the children could attend public school, my father, with the help of a few local Hispanics, built a two-story stone Opera House which still stands today. In this way, Narciso dreamed of bringing some class and culture to this unrefined part of the world. It was in the downstairs rooms of that structure that our family set up housekeeping.

No opera ever resounded off the walls of that fabulous building, other than the strains of the arias that emanated from Narciso's mouth as he worked. After all, this was cowboy country. Except for some of the other Italian immigrants, no one in that part of the world had ever heard of opera. The Grand Ole Opry wasn't even coming out of Nashville, Tennessee yet!

The structure was used as an athletic club for awhile and was soon adapted to provide a venue for the Chautauqua shows that traveled across the West in those days as well as a silent movie theater. Needless to say, I watched every movie that played in that large, upstairs room; sometimes from the front row of seats, and others propped on a stool in the projection booth next to my father. Mary Pickford became my idol and I grew up dreaming of becoming an actress just like her.

In addition to the films and dance bands that came through, public dances for both the Hispanics and the Anglos were held at the Opera House on alternate Saturday nights. The music from live orchestras—the jazz bands as well as the Spanish musicians—caught and held my imagination. Against this backdrop I learned the Spanish language, as well as the arts of acting and dancing, sometimes all three at the same time! By the time I was ten years of age I could sing songs in three languages: my mother-tongue of Italian, the Spanish of many of my friends and my father's customers, and the English that I was being taught in school. I liked to be in the school plays because I had watched with interest the dramas put on by the traveling Chautauqua actors.

The education and upbringing of a little immigrant child took on many tangents in those days. It was the kind of education that rubbed off on me like climbing through a sooty chimney. The sounds and smells and colors mingled into an array that was like a tapestry without a border or defined lines. The mingling of cultures, languages, and talents became one in my young soul.

I learned, for instance, about Thanksgiving and Christmas and Easter and the traditional ways in which those holidays were celebrated here in America. The turkey, pumpkin pie, and corn bread dressing were novelties in my home. Even though my mother tried to adapt to the new foods it wasn't natural for us, so the basis of the meals always remained the huge bowls of minestrone, the variety of pastas, and, of course, the traditional Italian polenta, or corn meal mush.

We laughed at the thought of Santa coming down a chimney with gifts, and a Christmas tree was unthinkable. Hanging stockings near the old coal and wood stove was awkward, but one Christmas morning I actually found a soft doll with a china head stuffed into one of them. At that moment I was transformed into a child of western America.

Hiding hard-boiled eggs in the empty field behind the Opera House seemed to be a strange way to celebrate the Resurrection of Jesus, but we went along with it. However, it was the new Easter ribbon tied to the end of my long, heavy braid that truly counted to me. Most importantly, my family enjoyed the religious aspects of Christmas and Easter and took part in the ceremonies at the little church across town.

The flickering, bright light of the Opera House's movie projector brought entertainment to many, but, after several years, the town doctor warned my father that he would lose his sight if he kept showing the silent movies. So, we sold the building to the Methodist Church, who hold services there to this day, and moved up the road to a small four-room house that my father built. By then, I was in the third grade at the school across the street, also built by Narciso. I immediately felt at home with the many Spanish-speaking children in that school because of my long association with our Spanish and Mexican customers at the dances and picture shows. The little house where we lived has become known as the "Grandma and Grandpa House," or simply the "G and G House," by my sons. My nephew, Mike, and his wife Margie still live in that memory-filled home. It was in those rooms, where I learned about life, and heard the stories of the Etruscans and the Old Country, where their daughter, named Divina after my mother, was raised, and learned the family history and the ways of this ever-changing world.

From Aida to the Hallelujah Chorus

The first structure built on the property that is now the Cimarron First Methodist Church was a two-room adobe hut with a flat, tar-papered roof covered with sand from the nearby stream. It was the first home of a young immigrant couple, Narciso and Divina Federici, my parents. They arrived in Cimarron, from Italy, in 1906, by way of Raton and Dawson, New Mexico.

Narciso was born in a small mountain town, Prota, in the foothills of the Italian Alps. As a young man he dreamed of coming to America. The woman of his dreams, Divina Mazzoni, also lived in Prota where they had grown up as neighbors and attended the same small church. Both of them had heard about that fabulous country where gold grew on trees like shining apples and how land in the frontier was being given to people if they would simply settle on it, grow crops, and build a home. And the best part, it was free! What a fabulous dream. But how could two people leave their homes, their families, and everything they had ever known to go across the world to start on that fantasy?

The Federici and Mazzoni families were poor people that lived off the land in that rocky part of the Alps. The only crops they had were grapes and chestnuts. One day Narciso walked to a neighboring town named Aulla where his family bought two things: salt and tobacco. They grew all the other few necessities they needed. Narciso stopped in a small cafe for food and drink and met a well-dressed Englishman who spoke a few words of Italian. He had come to Northern Italy to recruit stone masons. He had heard in Rome that in these isolated small towns in the north there were able-bodied men that knew masonry by working the Massa Carrara marble quarries.

Narciso had spent two summers at Massa Carrara and had found that the work was hard but rewarding. Then and there he signed on with the Englishman. All he knew was that he would get free transportation to a place called Egypt where they were building a dam across the Nile River at a place called Aswan.

Narciso was somewhat apprehensive about leaving Italy but the fact that he could get room and board and earn the money to go to America was all the incentive he needed. It all came true; Narciso traveled to Egypt, honed his skills as a stone mason while working side-by-side with men from all over the world building the dam in the middle of the desert. Eventually, he earned enough money for the move to America. He quit his job, and he went.

Upon arriving in America his first job was in the coal mines in Dawson, New Mexico, where he earned enough money to send for his sweetheart, Divina. In time, she too said goodbye to her family and friends and made the voyage to the new world and New Mexico. Narciso and Divina married and moved to Cimarron, 18 miles away from Dawson. Recruiting the help of several of the Hispanic men he had met in town he built an adobe hut that would be their first home. It was a marvel to the Italian couple that they could build a house with mud and straw instead of stones and lumber. It was a quick and easy method to build a shelter for them to live in, and it was cool in the summer and snug in the winter.

Divina laughed when they started shoveling dirt onto the water-proof tar paper used on the roof. She was sure she would drown in a shower of mud the first time they had a hard rain. Some seeds in the dirt they used for a roof sprouted and, before summer ended, there were huge sunflowers waving in the breeze overhead. These huge, wonderful flowers reminded Divina of the old country and helped to lift her spirits when she became lonely in this foreign land with strange languages and awkward, even crazy-seeming ways.

The cowboys she saw on the streets walked on long, wobbly legs when they got off their horses, spit some ugly black fluid out of their mouths, and blew their noses by holding one nostril closed and blowing out of the other; wiping their noses on the their shirt sleeves when they were done!

Soon Divina began to insist that Narciso quit his work in the dirty and dangerous mines and start his own business building homes and businesses in Cimarron. Narciso too had always believed that one should "never work for another if you can work for yourself." Because of his experience in Egypt he was able do just that. He put his masonry skills to work and began to earn a reputation as a builder of sturdy stone buildings. Several rich families from England, coming to find their future in America as well, had ended up in Cimarron over the years. They needed houses and Narciso knew that the local sandstone hills would provide all that he would need in terms of building material for handsome, strong homes. He opened a quarry above town and soon had all the work he could handle.

Soon he decided to take on a more ambitious project. He announced one day that he was going to build an Opera House. My mother was bewildered, "An opera house? You have never been in an opera house in your life or even heard a complete opera. You've only heard your friends sing arias from operas when you are in the tavern, or your own voice when you're taking a bath. You've only heard stories about that Opera House in Milan. And why would these people out here in the wilds of America want to go to the opera?"

Dad put his arm around his wife's shoulders and broke out singing in his good tenor voice. All she could do was shake her head and mumble to herself. She knew it would do no good to try and argue with this hard-headed husband.

I still weep to this day when I recognize a piece of an Italian opera on the radio or television that my dad used to sing while he worked. I realize now that he knew quite a few of the arias by heart. I always thought that most of them were tragic—it seems as if someone was always either dead or dying, or being betrayed.

Needless to say, the Opera House was built. It was a fine two-story stone structure that could hold up to 250 guests. All the guests were to enter by way of an outside staircase on the north side of the building where they would ascend to the auditorium on the second floor. Narciso built dressing rooms on either side of the curtained stage. The floor was made of hardwood, brought in especially from Denver. The lighting was provided by carbide lights. On the lower floor were the living quarters for our family, plus a large room with doors that opened to the south where the horse-drawn carriages were stored.

It was soon evident that my father had bit off more than he could chew. The Opera House was finished but, even if there was a willing audience, there were no singers, no impresarios, no managers, and no producers. I'm sure that, in his own mind, his dream became a nightmare. However, he never let on to the rest of us. He had set out to build an opera house in little Cimarron, New Mexico, and "by Gott" he had done it!

Growing up in that huge barn-like building, my brothers, my sister, and I, instead of being treated to operas in our house, my father offered instead Chautauqua traveling shows, Saturday night dances, and the silent movies of Charlie Chaplin and Mary Pickford. Down through the years we still call it "The Opera House," but it was also used as a roller skating rink and an athletic hall, complete with a phonograph player for music and wooden bar bells for weight lifting. A commercial laundry was also installed on the lower floor where several women scrubbed away their days on washing boards over steaming tubs of water. In the backyard, the clotheslines were always full and busy, fresh white linens blowing in the dry, southwestern breeze.

Dancing was held frequently in the Opera House. The Anglos and the Hispanics of the town did not often mix other than at work and at school, so they held their dances on alternate Saturdays. Both brought their own music and their own food. The only beverage available was coffee, of which gallons were drunk; there were no alcoholic beverages or sodas at the time.

After a few years, Narciso found that he was having trouble with his eyes because of the bright flickering light of the projector that was used to show the silent films. His doctor in Raton advised him that he might become blind if he continued, so he decided to sell the Opera House. He found a buyer and sold the place to a Methodist preacher named Traveller. Narciso built a new home just up the street, and the family moved. My nephew, Mike, and his wife Margie still live in that house; his daughter Divina having grown up in the same rooms that I had run and played in as a child.

Narciso was sorry to see the fruits of his first dream become something other than what he had envisioned, however he could see other dreams coming over the horizon, and he knew his children would play an important part in those future dreams. I really don't think he was overly disappointed. His future, and that of his family, unfolded in the following years in ways that made him proud. Proud of his Italian heritage, and proud to be an American. The ideas and dreams that had spawned on the Nile River in Egypt, and during his youth in Italy, blossomed here in New Mexico. He lived to see his children become well-educated and respected in their chosen fields in an alien land. The two sons, Fred and Bill, became lawyers and judges and my sister, Emma, and I married men who became successful in the fields of education and as a businessman.

On Sunday mornings, as you pass by the big stone Cimarron Methodist Church and you listen as the voices of the choir and congregation waft out of the open windows as they sing the Hallelujah Chorus, listen hard. Among those voices, if you listen carefully enough, you will hear the voice of a tenor, singing loud and strong. My father, too, had many reasons to "Praise the Lord."

Blackie

We named her Blackie. She was left at our home in Cimarron late one night. It was customary at that time that if someone had something they didn't want, they just dropped it at someone's front door. Sometimes it was a kitten, a duck, or a chicken, and it could even be a baby wrapped up in a cotton blanket.

Blackie was a small pup with long black hair, and not a single white hair on her little body. Even though the only food she ever received from us was the soup bones from the minestrone that my mother made for the family, she grew up quickly with sturdy, fat legs. Minestrone is a thick, hearty vegetable soup made with whatever vegetables were ripe in the garden, but the one thing it always had in it was a good beef bone for flavor. Blackie could always count on the bone from the minestrone to be set out after dinner near the big rusty bucket that always sat under the garden pump; the pump that leaked and dripped all year round, keeping the bucket full at all times.

In those days we used to drive the old Overland to the Ranch at Apache Hill once or twice every week to build fence around the 125 acres, or to hoe the corn, beans, and squash that we grew there. It was part of the rules we had to observe in order to "prove up" and earn the ownership of a Homestead in the West as part of the arrangement to receive the free land in the beautiful, wonderful land of America.

We never took Blackie with us when we left the house; she was left behind with a bone or two and the bucket of running water which was apparently all she needed, for she was always there to greet us when we returned. One day, however, the five of us in the family packed up the car with some food and left Cimarron to go to Apache Hill for a few days. We were at the Ranch for almost three days on this particular trip, and when we arrived home in the late evening, we did not receive our usual happy greeting and wagging tail from Blackie. To our dismay when we opened the front door, we found Blackie cowering in the corner of the kitchen, and we found to our horror that all the wallpaper had been torn down from all the walls and halls of our five room home.

I ran to Blackie and led her outdoors to the cold bucket of water and she plunged her nose deep into it and drew long gulps of the cold water and coughed and groaned in the effort to quench her thirst. Then I returned to the house and found my mother, Divina, moaning and wailing as she ran from room to room surveying the damage and then gazing skyward, with her hands uplifted in a prayerful motion and tears streaming from her eyes.

That's when my father walked to the garage, got a small rope, and retuned to the house and got his loaded shotgun. He tied the rope around Blackie's neck and they both walked up one of the arroyos at the back of the house that we called Wonder Ditch. My brothers and sisters and I clung to my mother's skirt and it wasn't long until we heard the report of the gun in the quiet of the evening. We knew what had happened, and were terrified, but no one uttered a sound. My mother walked to the kitchen and in a short period of time she placed a large cauldron of warmed-over minestrone and five bowls with spoons on the table. Still there was no sound of crying or mourning or sadness in the room.

We all sat at the table and ate hungrily at the soup and hard crusts of French bread. After dinner we all went to our separate sleeping quarters and I wept quietly under the bed cover.

Part of me knew I should hate my father. But I had been there during the weeks of labor at night when we all worked together to paper that house, covering the greasy and dirty planks of wood, and the cracks in the walls to let the cold wind blow through in the winter. Lying there, I recalled my father standing on the ladder, holding the rolls of cut wallpaper in his hands. My mother would be standing below him holding up the paper which kept falling down on her beautiful auburn hair and getting it caught in the fresh paste that I had made on the stove out of flour and water.

My job had been to brush the paste onto the backside of the wallpaper and try not to drip too much of it down on my mother's head and shoulders. I remember keeping a large pair of scissors nearby to cut off any of my mother's hair that would get caught in the paste, and I remember thinking what a pity it was to have to do that to my mother's beautiful hair. And yet, I thought what a wonderful thing it would be to have some of my mother's hair to keep—which I would cherish forever.

I also remember thinking of my father's tired arms, having come home from a long day working as a stone mason building the walls for new homes all over town; laying the large, heavy, cut stones in place as the walls rose higher, and now, in the evenings, having to hold the heavy paper in place over his head.

Did I hate my father? Yes, I think I hated him that first night after the incident with Blackie. But, I was there and I understood the agony and work that had gone into the wall papering, especially when it was after a hard day's labor. I came to realize after I grew up that although hatred can provide relief, it doesn't actually cure anything. I knew the hate my father must have had in his heart when he took Blackie to the arroyos. I also realized that hate can come in a black flash that can ruin a person's life forever if you can't understand and forgive.

Forgiveness, as with love, is a virtue that must become a part of our lives. In Italian the word 'Personae' plays a large part in everyday life. One of my mother's favorite proverbs which she quoted often to me was: 'Perdonare á molto valore.' But sometimes in the middle of the night I keep thinking, "what a price little Blackie paid for the privilege of that rusty bucket of cold water!"

All For The Glory of a Taste Bud

I have been involved with food and the preparation of it since I was ten years old. When I was a child my mother had to help my father in the General Store that we owned in a spot named Colfax, New Mexico. The store was open for business practically 24 hours a day and took care of many of the needs for the families scattered around us in a twenty-five mile area.

Since the population was made up of coal miners, ranch owners and road-way construction crews we had to carry quite a variety of food, clothes, and even medical supplies. The customers came in trucks, wagons, and even on horseback. The red chili ristras we carried were equally as important as the tooth ache medicine, or the chewing tobacco, or the dry yeast, potatoes and cabbage.

I remember the day my little sister was born on a Sunday morning in the two rooms in the back of the country store that we called home. Dr. Bass had to come all the way from Cimarron, twelve miles away, to help with the birth. Even though I was almost ten years old, I had no idea until that day that my mother was pregnant. In those days women did not flaunt their pregnancies. It was almost as if they were ashamed of the fact, and they wore huge skirts and blouses to hide it, and young children had no idea that a new life was in progress.

As a result, I was very concerned and frightened when I walked into our kitchen and heard and saw all the excitement coming from the bedroom in the next room. I was surprised to find my mother in bed and right next to the bed was a handmade cradle made from a wooden case which had previously held a collection of jelly beans, orange sugar clusters, and peanut brittle in glass candy canisters for the customers to choose from.

I looked down into the box which had now been covered on the inside with cotton flannel from the store and tucked into the sides to keep the new little customer clean, and warm and happy. The red-faced, squirming creature that I beheld was not exactly pretty, or happy. My Aunt Julia who had dropped in from their quarters next door was fussing around with hot water and squares of flannel which I found out quickly were the first of the many diapers that I would be washing for months on end and hanging from the clothesline behind the store to dry.

I was then introduced to my new sister, Emma, and she seemed too fragile and helpless for anyone like me to take care of. Yet, in addition to having to cook for the family and keep the dishes washed up and the beds clean while my parents tended to business, I soon learned to bathe the little creature, and learned how to fold the cotton square so it would fit snugly around that red body with the two skinny legs that kept kicking and thrashing around like those of a little frog in a pond of water. For some reason Emma did not like my mother's milk and the minute she swallowed a few gulps of it, some of it running down her little cheek, she became colicky and very uncomfortable. We quickly realized that we would have to find something else to keep her nourished, happy, and alive. We had heard that the Mexicans in the area used a type of canned milk that we sold in the store by carloads. Apparently you could boil some water to mix in with the sticky yellow syrup and feed it to babies two or three times a day and they thrived on it.

Emma was no exception and she soon became a fat, chubby, healthy little baby. We also learned to add something else to the milk, something in powdered form, that would keep her from becoming bow-legged later when she would start standing and walking on her own.

And that is how I started to learn about food and the preparation of it at an early age. Living in the back of a country store made it easy for me to walk into the front of the building and get the meats, vegetables, and fruits to cook with. I remember I never cooked things like steak or pork chops or lamb chops that sold well to our customers, but rather I was encouraged to get some of the things that weren't selling well, and by adding the right herbs, seasonings, and vegetables I could make something to please everyone at the end of the day. The hardest and most trying part of the day was to cook the polenta; a staple of Italians made with corn meal. With one good chicken and a pot of polenta we could feed dozens, young or old.

Many years later when I found myself as a grown woman in Australia, I could not help but remember how it was cooking in the back part of a country store in New Mexico. I had come a long way since then and, having married a college professor who was lecturing in many parts of the world, I found that no matter where you found yourself, people and food went together, and, that you could learn a lot about the different cultures just by smelling the foods.

And so it was that I found myself one afternoon attending an International Buffet in Tasmania, Australia in a town named Hobart. All the food there reminded me of what the Duke of Edinburgh once said about good food—and he should know what he is talking about; "there is only one trouble about food as far as I am concerned—a little of what I fancy seems to go such a long way." That wonderful buffet also reminded me of an exhibition of fine foods that I had attended there in Hobart shortly after we had arrived; however, there was a difference. That difference was that the Australians included wines as well as foods of many nations.

It was arranged by a committee to raise funds for the Girl Guides Association of Tasmania, who, in company with Guides throughout the world, was raising money to build an International Guides hostel at Poons in India. They announced that international hostels already existed in London, Mexico and Switzerland and the committee said that any move which fosters goodwill between nations should be worthy of support.

I remember that one of the most outstanding exhibits that day was the table exhibiting a Wedding Buffet featuring the combined art of many of Hobart's leading hotel chefs. Other tables displayed food and settings of the Victorian and Old English eras. European and Eastern countries as well as a special Children's Party table were among the many tables. A large collection of special cakes were on sale. Australian, as well as international, wines and a great variety of interesting ingredients were exhibited, as well as many fine books about food and its preparation. You could even have tastes of the food and wine. Attractive flower arrangements added to the beauty of the Town Hall and the Exhibition.

I thought it would interest you that women are women everywhere, and that food, and its preparation and serving for worthy causes, goes on in many strange and faraway corners of the globe. However, an interesting sidelight of this Food Exhibition in Hobart came to my attention and caused me to chuckle. One of my new friends in Hobart had a young daughter who attended a Catholic boarding school in Hobart. She wrote a note to her parents telling them that her entire class visited the Exhibition. She said in her letter that they were not allowed to taste the meat because it was Friday, there were too many of them for lemonade, and they were too young for the wine. According to the girl's father, "it was more or less a case of too religious, too many, and too young!"

The Art of Capturing
a Special Moment

Capturing a special moment in our lives is a lot like capturing a beautiful butterfly in a net. Putting that moment down on paper will keep it alive forever. Of course, a butterfly can only be enjoyed for a short period of time as compared with an incident in one's life, but even with a butterfly, the gossamer beauty of color and design will last forever in memory.

A life is made up of fleeting moments wrapped up in an empty cone or shell. Some of the moments are meaningless and some last forever, depending on what you do with them. The following story was an important part of my life that I like to remember and dwell upon.

It was Mrs. Pochel who was my teacher in a one room school house in Colfax, New Mexico who first taught me the importance of putting my thoughts down on paper.

She taught grades 1 through 8 in the little school built on the top of a rocky hill not far from my home. There was no library in the school however every weekend she would bring loads of books from her home town of Las Vegas, New Mexico and at the beginning of each week my fellow students and would fight over them. Also every Monday morning we would prepare little one-act plays that we would put on for our parents when they came to the school.

It was through her books that I first learned about art and writing and Greek and Roman history. For the small children in our one-room school house she brought huge charts that could be rolled up and put away when not in use. As I developed into the Fifth and Sixth grades, I took my turn with a long pointer and helped the small children with their first lessons in reading. In those days, it was very important to teach reading by sounds and pronunciation especially since so many of the children were of mixed ethnic backgrounds, and for whom English was not a first language.

Mrs. Pochel would play the piano that lived in the old school and teach us all of the early nursery rhymes and children's songs for Christmas, Easter, and Fourth of July. We were even taught our numbers by music. It was in this school that I was introduced to, and given, my first tooth brush, which was purchased and brought to the school by the County School Superintendent. She also had a hand-cranked phonograph record player she would crank while we did a half hour of exercise to music every morning before classes began.

Ernesto Finds a Wife

I knew Ernesto as long as I can remember. He was like a second father to me. My earliest recollection of Ernesto was that he was a kind and gentle man with a low, soft voice. He laughed often, and I liked to sit on his lap and curl his long mustache upward until it looked like the miniature horns of a billy goat.

Ernesto was a distant cousin that had come to join the family in New Mexico from the same part of Italy that my parents had come from years before. He helped cut the stone with which my father, Narciso, was going to build an opera house in order to bring some civilization to this desolate and rough part of the world. My father never tired of talking about the culture he would introduce to these "barbarians" who only knew of swinging doors, pistols, and "rot-gut whiskey," and Ernesto never tired of listening.

"Why, they don't even know how to blow their noses!" Narciso would say. "Instead of a handkerchief, they hold one side of their noses and blow into the wind and onto the street!" As he told his stories, and explained his philosophies of life, he would light a match to the Toscano cigar and the smoke would drift across the kitchen ceiling to mingle with the odor of the garlic that was being sautéed in the olive oil in preparation for the spaghetti sauce for dinner. Ernesto would laugh his quiet laugh. He never seemed to have any clever things to say, like Narciso, but he always enjoyed listening to his friend's stories and commentary.

Ernesto was unmarried and almost thirty years old and it was a common belief among the people of the village that the time had come for him to marry, start his own family, and have a home of his own. The problem was, however, that in this small town in New Mexico there were only a half-dozen Italian families from which to seek a wife, and many of these were young couples who were just starting families of their own. There were simply no young Italian women of marriageable age in the community.

There were available women who would have been happy to marry Ernesto, however they were either Mexican, Spanish, or Indian, or mixtures of those three cultures. Many of them were fantastically beautiful, with their large brown-black eyes, full, sensuous lips, and raven-black hair that had never been cut. They were full of life, loved to dance and sing, and made wonderful cooks and mothers. And yet, although Ernesto was tempted, he was shy about getting involved with any of them, especially since it was so hard to communicate his thoughts and plans. He had not had the opportunity to learn English or Spanish because he spoke only Italian during the day with the men in the hills cutting stone, and in the evening, he spent time talking with Narciso's family about the old days in Italy.

My father had a brother who had also come to America and settled in the local coal mining town of Dawson. Guido was his name, and he was a tailor by trade. He and his wife and three daughters would occasionally come to see Narciso and my family and spend the day. There would be much eating, drinking of wine, talking, and laughing, and the children fought and screamed and yelled, as children do. On one of their visits, Guido suggested that he and Narciso should return to Italy to see their aging parents, and to sell their small pieces of property with the chestnut trees and grapevines to relatives in Prota. The brothers could use the money to build their homes in America and send their children to school.

Narciso, having had more than his share of wine that afternoon, agreed instantly with Guido that it was a terrific idea. He did not stop to think about the fact that he was in the middle of helping to construct a huge, two-story stone building in town, or that his wife and three children would have to be left behind. Later, after Guido and his family had departed for their home and my family had settled into bed, I could hear my parents discussing the subject late into the night.

"But, Narciso, how can we manage without you here?" my mother argued. "You have five men working at the quarry and constructing the walls of the opera house. I have to board the men, which I can manage, but can the men manage without you? Do they know how to cut the stone properly for those large windows and doors? The stone has to be cut so precisely and set into those walls in just the right way. Can they do that without you?"

Narciso knew that his wife had a point, but he also knew that this might be the last opportunity of his lifetime to go back to the place of his birth. He finally came up with the idea that his cousin Ernesto could help. Ernesto was a man of experience in stone-cutting and building. He had had the same training as Narciso working in the hills of Massa Carrara, not far from their home in Italy, where huge blocks of marble were cut for the buildings and statues in the far off cities of Florence and Rome.

"Ernesto knows as much about the work as I do, and maybe even more," Narciso said to his wife. "Guido and I will only be gone for two or three months. It's my last chance. Guido can loan me the cash for the trip, and I'll pay him back when the opera house is opened up and we are in business."

Gradually, my mother, Divina, was convinced that, perhaps, this would be a good idea after all. Because of her responsibilities she knew she would not be able to go with Narciso, but maybe her chance would come after the children were grown and married. She knew she likely would never again see her own parents, but this was something she had faced the day she left them behind to come to this wild, savage, and uncivilized land to be with Narciso—the man she loved.

More than two months passed before all the preparations for the trip were completed and the proper papers had been obtained. Guido had made two fine suits, one for himself and one for his brother, Narciso, so they could go back home with the look of prosperity upon them.

Ernesto watched these preparations closely and had become very interested in their plans. One evening, Narciso joked to Ernesto that he would bring back an Italian wife for him. At first Ernesto blushed at the joke, but the more they thought about it, the more it seemed like a sound idea. Unfortunately, Ernesto had no particular woman in mind back home, and the one he had left behind had found a husband from the nearby village of Aulla within a year after Ernesto's departure. The subject was dropped, however both men continued to privately consider the possibility of a suitable wife being found in the Old Country. Soon, in early spring, Narciso and Guido left for their homeland.

When the two brothers arrived in Italy, and made their way to the little rocky, hilltop town of Prota, all work stopped for ten days as the friends and relatives gathered from all over the surrounding area to hear the stories of America. The brothers caught up on all the family news and ate and drank too much, as was required. It was a wonderful homecoming for the two Federici boys. At these gatherings, Narciso kept a sharp look-out for a proper wife for Ernesto. He spread the word around the valley that he was looking for a young woman to take back with him to America as a wife for his friend Ernesto.

America! As soon as the mothers of Prota heard about Narciso's quest, they began to vie with each other to have the brothers in for dinner. The young ladies of the families dressed in their finest clothes and helped their mothers serve the dinners to the two worldly Federici men. All of them wanted to make a good impression on Narciso. It became a contest to see who would be chosen as the potential wife for Ernesto. Who would be considered as the woman to be taken across the wide ocean to America?

The weeks flew past. When it was almost time for the brothers to return to America, Narciso had narrowed his choice to the three eligible daughters of the Mazzoni family. All three were hard-working young women, he thought, who had taken on the farm work of their few rocky acres after their father had died. They had strong arms and legs, and their complexions were bronzed from working in the fields. They wore kerchiefs on their heads that were tied at the nape of their necks; underneath the kerchiefs, abundant dark hair struggled to be released and cascade in profusion down their backs.

It was going to be a difficult decision. Each one was as strong and healthy and fresh looking as her sister. There was only one difference among them. The youngest had a slight cast in one eye. Because of this minor flaw, it had become accepted that she would have a more difficult time finding a husband in her own hometown. She should have the opportunity to go to America where there was a lonely, homesick man who would love and cherish her. Marietta would be the one!

About a week before the brothers were to depart, Narciso called his friends and relatives together at his old home in Prota, which was situated just below the old church that he had attended as a boy. In preparation for the meeting, the stone piazza was swept clean, jugs of wine were placed conveniently on the tables, and roasted and boiled chest-nuts filled bowls of all sizes and colors. Cheeses and large, fragrant loaves of bread, and long, dark salamis were scattered on the tables with knives to cut and slice them.

The time had come to make the announcement. There was a feeling of expectation as well as sadness in the air of the little mountain village. When Narciso stood up on the elevated stone wall, he must have felt a bit like an old Roman orator preparing to make his speech to the populace. After clearing his throat and making a few clever remarks, Narciso asked for the attention of all. He thanked the gathering for their wonderful hospitality, wished them good luck in the future, and expressed the hope that a few of them would someday join their relatives in the little town in New Mexico.

He repeated what he had said in the weeks and months before about this faraway land: it was a wild, hard land, so different from this village in Italy. It was an arid country with no grapes, chestnuts, or olive trees. One could travel for days and not meet another human being. The people who lived there were helpful and friendly enough, especially if you had a trade that could be used, but they kept to themselves. There were no doctors or hospitals or churches nearby. It was difficult to communicate to anyone what you needed or wanted since they spoke a strange language. And, until now, there was not an opera house to be found.

Narciso stepped off the stone wall and walked over to where the Mazzoni daughters sat in the cool shade with their aged mother. He placed his arms around the young woman, Marietta, who shyly lifted her face and looked up at him. She reminded him of Mochi's sculpture Annunciation, a statue of a virgin that he had seen once in Orvieto. Looking down into Marietta's eyes, Narciso felt that Mochi must have had someone in mind much like her when he lifted that image from the cold marble.

Narciso announced to the gathering that he and Guido would like to have Marietta accompany them to the New World; America. Everyone clapped and cheered. Marietta felt as if she had been touched by a magic wand. But, with all the celebration, there were many tears shed and a lot of hugging and crying among the old people; knowing they were about to say goodbye to yet another of their own.

Just over a week later, Marietta kissed her parents and sisters goodbye, forever, picked up her small, tattered suitcase, and followed Narciso and Guido down the road that wound away from Prota and everything she had ever known. The three Italian countrymen found their way to Spain where they boarded the steamer ship that would carry them across the Atlantic Ocean to where they would let the train carry them even further away; to the beginning of a new chapter in their life in America.

By the time they boarded the train in New York, Narciso had become confidant that he had made the right choice with Marietta. He had become comfortable with, and accustomed to the shortcomings of the young woman's physical appearance. The flatness of her facial features had come to seem, somehow, attractive to him. He found that he was noticing the unusual cast in her left eye less and less as the days, and miles, washed by. He was sure now that she would be a good woman. She was strong and never hesitated to help when it came to lifting their baggage onto a cart or train. At the ship's dinner table, she always served the men first out of the huge bowls of strange soups and stews that appeared out of the galley, and then herself and the few other women on board.

Narciso recognized in her a woman who would add to Ernesto's life the things that he needed; hearty and delicious meals to come home to after his hard days at the quarry, or on the scaffolds at one of the new buildings they would be constructing; someone to be with during the long winter nights; someone who spoke the same language as Ernesto, with whom he could share his dreams, and fears, and the memories of the Old Country.

Nonetheless, Narcisco became more and more anxious the closer the three of them got to New Mexico and the awaiting groom-to-be. Although Ernesto had been told that Narciso and Guido were on their way home, and that a young woman was coming with them to be his future wife, he knew little more.

Therefore, when the train pulled into the station in Raton, New Mexico several weeks after leaving the little village in northern Italy, Ernesto stood quietly apart from Divina and the others that had come from Cimarron to welcome the travelers home. His hands fidgeted in the pockets of the new pair of pants he had worn. His eyes failed to meet those of the others, whose eyes were mostly on him.

At last, he saw Narciso step down from the train and onto the wooden platform. Then, Guido. Divina walked slowly to Narciso's side where she quietly took his arm in her hands. Three other women stepped down from the passenger car, but they were old, much older than Ernesto; surely none of these could be his bride. Finally, a strong-looking woman of the right age appeared. She held her eyes to the ground but walked purposefully to Narcisco where she and Divina hugged, having not seen each other in what seemed like a life time. Then her face lifted. Over Divina's shoulder she saw a man she recognized from her days as a little girl, growing up in Prota. Ernesto, with no show of emotion other than a quiet, muted fear, looked back at her. From a life of experiencing it, she recognized the glance that his dark eyes made to one side of her face as they focused on her left eye, the one with the cast. They then moved back to look her squarely in both eyes, and there they stayed.

Divina stepped aside to allow Narciso to make the introduction. As they heard each other's name, they nodded, unsmiling and somber. Then, Ernesto took Marietta's hand and led her toward the other side of the building where the cars were parked.

The years that followed their marriage made Marietta comfortably thankful for having been chosen as the one to share Ernesto's life here in America. She always knew, in her heart, the reason that she had been selected to be his wife. She was always aware that Narciso's final decision had been based on the fact that she was facing the likelihood of living her life out as a single woman in Italy. There were not many young, unmarried men left in the villages from where she came, and those that had stayed were pairing up with the prettier girls, like her sisters.

Ernesto also knew, that without the arrival of Marietta, the chances of him finding a woman here, in the remoteness of New Mexico, that could fill the empty spaces in his life and fulfill his needs as an Italian immigrant in a world apart from the one he knew, were slim.

It wasn't love that kept Ernesto and Marietta together. Not at first. Yet their love grew each day, and each night. The mere fact that Ernesto was thankful and happy to have her near him for the rest of his life made that love real for Marietta. There were few ways available to her in which to repay the happiness that he brought into her life. Every morning as she stoked up the wood stove and prepared a simple breakfast, she found herself wanting to please Ernesto even more than the day before.

"Ernesto, what are you going to do today?" she would ask over the eggs and ham. "It's your day off; don't you think we should plant more vegetables in our garden? I think we need more cauliflower, cabbage, and endive, don't you?"

Ernesto would simply look into her eyes and smile. Of course she knew that these were his favorite vegetables, and she knew just how to prepare the polenta to go alongside of them. Perhaps with a turtle dove stew and gravy.

Fully Dressed and in My Right Mind

I was born of Catholic parents and raised in a Methodist town.

The Methodist Church was originally Narciso's Opera House, which he built shortly after he arrived there in 1903. Narcisco and Divina had come to America with hordes of other immigrants who thronged to this country of promises—promises of freedoms they did not enjoy in their own countries; freedom to worship and live as they preferred, freedom to use the muscles in their backs and arms to make a decent living, freedom to educate their children in the American schools, to learn this new language and the ways of these new, rigorous, active pioneers.

My father was an adjustable man and knew that, with God willing, he would soon be raising a family and they would need shelter and food and clothing. That's why he thought that an opera house would be a sensible venture here in this culture-starved corner of the Frontier West. However, the people out there were not interested in Italian arias, not even as a break from the hard work and monotony of their pioneer lives. So, Narcisco had to change his dreams.

One day a young frontier lawyer from England suggested to my father that there were many other possible uses for the beautiful, two-story stone building. He told my father that in England they had Athletic Clubs where the young men could gather after work for exercise. So my father took his suggestion seriously and the Opera House became the Cimarron Athletic Club. However, before long, the work-outs had given way to dance bands, traveling Chautauqua shows, and silent movies.

At times, young people from the area and nearby ranches and gold mining towns paid small dues to rent the top floor. I remember watching the beautiful young Americans come on horseback or buggies drawn by horses and they moved the theater chairs from the top floor and cleaned and washed the scuffed floor until it shone. They made little sleeping and eating places out of the dressing rooms with chairs and tables and bead curtains. It was almost like watching the preparation for a Shakespearian play or an old-fashioned musical comedy.

My father's house was an active, exciting place, especially for a little girl. My life at what the family still calls "The Opera House" was a wonderful educational experience for a young girl. And it was a clean and respectful environment. Wives and husbands respected each other and the young were well behaved and generally under the supervision of the older people. As my father used to say, "The young should always be fully dressed and in their right minds."

Groups of Chautauqua Players, originating from Chautauqua, New York, would come and stay for a week, perform their play or musicals, and then move on while another group arrived and replaced them. The Chautauqua Players that passed through brought their own pre-rehearsed plays and their own stage props. All they needed from us was a proper theater arrangement with chairs, stage, curtains, and of course, a piano; the only instrument that the Players couldn't carry with them around the country. My father had a piano sent from Denver to fill the need. It was a player piano as well as a regular piano. Sometimes, if we were short handed, I was asked to pump the piano pedals to drive the magic rollers through it and make the keys jump and the music rise from the strings for the production.

Occasionally, if they needed a child in the play, the players would script me in. I was instructed what to do and say. I loved the attention I received and I loved the applause! As I recall, some of the parts I played were "Little Miss Muffett" or "Little Orphan Annie", or they just taught me some simple tap dances and I loved those and can still dance to some of that music when I hear it.

The family lived in a portion of the ground floor of the Opera House. The center of our lives was, of course, the kitchen. It served not only as a place for the preparation and eating of food, but also as what we would now call the living room. We lived entirely in that room except for when we were sleeping.

In one corner stood the old Happy Home coal and wood stove, the center of all the activity. It was very important to keep enough wood and coal on hand, for that stove not only kept us warm on cold nights, but it also heated the water that we needed to keep clean and cook our meals.

Wood was easy to come by; we had only to walk or ride a few miles from home and the hills were covered with dead, dry trees and wood scattered all over the ground. My father could load up the wagon on each of several days in the fall and bring home enough wood to keep us warm and fed through the whole year. The coal, on the other hand, was another thing. Coal was desirable because with a good chunk of coal you could keep the house warm all night or heat water for a whole day's washing.

Fortunately for us, we had a small train that came to Cimarron almost every day from Raton, New Mexico, carrying supplies and people going up to the gold mining communities and the ranches. This train was run entirely by coal from the local mines. There was a coal storage shed in Cimarron, not far from the Opera House, so every morning after breakfast or on weekends when I entered grade school, one of my jobs for the day was to walk across the railroad tracks to the shed and pick up coal that had fallen on the ground in the process of filling the coal tender cars on the trains.

I would fill my ten pound empty lard bucket and return to my home with my load. If I didn't get a full bucket at the shed, I walked along the railroad tracks and found more pieces of coal that had fallen off the train.

In those days when we did not have hair driers, it was a problem to dry our hair after washing it in large pans with water heated on the stove. There was no plumbing and the washing of anything was done in zinc wash tubs and the water thrown outdoors to our side of the front yard to water the new trees and bushes planted there. In the winter, we would dry our freshly washed hair in front of the open oven door of that stove. In the summer, however, when the stove was heated up only for meal preparation, we had to dry our hair in the backyard of the Opera House; out of view of passerby. In those days, a woman or even girl-child never let her hair hang down loose in public. It had to be braided and looped or on top of her head. Only at night before going to bed could a woman let her hair down and brush it to fall over her shoulders and down her back or the sides of her body.

The corner near the stove was always warmer than the other parts of the home. That corner was reserved for babies, sick children, or the elderly who would sit there and keep an eye on the children, peel potatoes, snap green beans or do the knitting or patching of socks or other clothes. It was in that corner that many quilts were made by hand from bundles of worn out clothing. Nothing was ever thrown out. All the remnants were used. I hardly remember a time when my mother didn't have a large, heavy, partially-finished quilt going on in that corner of that kitchen, or a basket of knitting, or even a large tub of wild turkeys or chickens ready to pluck and cook for dinner.

There was no indoor plumbing, so we had outdoor privies usually with two compartments—one for women and one for men. We did not have the luxury of soft absorbent toilet paper, so we saved the outdated Montgomery Ward or Sears and Roebuck catalogs and placed one in each of the outhouse compartments. A lot of my education and my brothers' education about underwear and the difference in the bodies between men and women came from those catalogs as we browsed through them while in the outhouse. As I recall, women in those days wore a lot of strange harnesses with pulleys and sashes and supports. It was as if they were embarrassed by the softness and natural curves of their bodies and tried to hide them or suppress them with their undergarments, which must have been very uncomfortable. Even in High School my mother made me wear tight girdles except when I was asleep in bed. She said it protected our backs and kept my female organs protected in order to have healthy babies someday!

For vegetables we depended almost entirely on our own garden plot behind the Opera House. The ground was turned every Spring and Fall by hand. That job fell to the women and, often, any visiting guests helped with that. The main things that came out of our garden were: onions, garlic, parsley, basil, cabbage, celery, peppers, lettuce, spinach, green beans, peas and tomatoes. Apples were our main food as far as fruit was concerned. Of course we had no oranges, lemons, or bananas. Sometimes we had grapes and peaches brought into town by trucks from Texas or Colorado.

My mother also made her own soap in that kitchen. I'm not sure what all of the ingredients that went into it, but I remember them talking about lye and fat. I didn't like the smell of the coarse, square blocks of soap as it was being prepared, however, everything was made soft and comfortable and pleasing by the wonderful olive oil my mother would add. She poured it out of large five-gallon tin containers that were sold to us by an Italian merchant in nearby Raton, New Mexico named DeLisio. He imported the olive oil from Italy along with polenta flour in large 50 lb. bags, dry parmesan cheese, goat milk, chestnuts, and dry cod fish which came in flat, light wooden crates.

The cod fish had to be soaked in water for several days to get the salt out of it. My mother made wonderful fried cod dipped in breadcrumbs, Parmesan cheese, and chopped onion and garlic. She also made a salad with boiled codfish, fresh onions, chopped celery, peppers with a dressing of olive oil, vinegar, salt, and pepper.

At Christmas time, special treats would appear in that kitchen. My favorites were roasted chestnuts along with hot wine which we would have when we arrived home after Christmas Eve Mass. Even the children could have a small cup of the wine which had been brought to a boil on the kitchen stove with a little sugar in it. When it started to boil, it was set afire with a kitchen match until all the alcohol had burned out. As I recall, it was heavenly and it made me very sleepy so I was tucked into my rough pallet made of chicken and turkey feathers. My bed was snuggled into a corner of the unheated laundry room off of the kitchen. Despite the chill in that room on winter nights, with feathers under me and a couple of mom's heavy woolen quilts on top, I was "snug as a bug in a rug."

My first Christmas tree was in that kitchen. The Italian culture did not use Christmas trees but my brothers and I had come home from school with tales of Christmas trees so my father cut down a small piñon pine tree from the nearby hillside and propped it up on a wooden block. I will never forget the happiness I felt when I found a straw stuffed doll with a china head riding in one of the branches of that piñon tree on Christmas morning!

Easter, on the other hand, was different for me than the one my American schoolmates shared. We did not boil and color or hide Easter eggs. We went to church at the little Catholic Church in Old Town across the Cimarron River. We were always happy when Easter Day came around because we were sick of eating codfish and cabbage salad on Sundays. We were anxious to have mom's good chicken stew and beef minestra and several hot slices of polenta made in an old pot reserved for that purpose

On the first day of school I was taken to the stone school house across the street from my home. I was very excited and had on a new dress my mother had made for the occasion. I lined up with all the other children and waited for the ringing of the hand bell that that would call us into the front entrance of the school. My heart pounded with excitement. I was finally going to be among children of my own age. Soon, a large gray-haired, stone-faced woman came out of the school and walked down the line of children looking at us. She stopped in front of me, grabbed my shoulder, and took me out of the line. "You're not old enough to be in school!" she said gruffly. "I can tell. You go home and tell your mother to come see me and bring your birth certificate."

I was saddened and chagrined. I chewed on my fingernails, hung my head, and slowly walked across the street and down the lane to the Opera House and home. I felt dirty and ashamed. It was another year before I was able to join that happy land of laughing children, and queer languages, and strange games.

Wonder Ditch

Every child should have his own Wonder Ditch. A Wonder Ditch is a certain private spot on Earth where you can go and connect with nature or contemplate your problems concerning your family, or teachers at school, or even your close friends.

I had my Wonder Ditch not far from the family home in Cimarron. It was actually a group of old arroyos, rather than a man-made ditch. But that's what I called it...my Wonder Ditch. It wasn't until I grew up that I found out that they call the state of New Mexico the "Land of Enchantment"; however I knew, from my days playing in those arroyos as a child, that the place was truly enchanted.

When I wasn't in school, I spent a lot of my free time playing in Wonder Ditch. Each year the flood waters would come down from the high mountains after a heavy rain and make my ditch deeper and wider and, in the process, uncover many things that I had never seen before. One of the things my inquisitive eyes and hands discovered in that ditch was that there had been someone living there long before my parents came to settle from Tuscany, Italy.

But I kept my interesting finds to myself and hid them in a natural cave in the side of one of the sandy walls of the Wonder Ditch. At one time I had dozens of ancient Indian pot shards and arrow heads cached there, and even the skeleton of a child; its wide open eye holes in the bony head looking up at me in wonder to be out in the sunshine again and getting acquainted with this immigrant child from clear across the world.

That little American Indian and I had some things in common. One was that we were born in that place that was eventually named "Cimarron"—meaning "untamed" or "lawless"—by the Spanish when they first came to the area. By the time I lived there it was just another quiet little New Mexican town where the language was mostly Spanish.

However, in school in those days, the teacher would crack you hard on the knuckles with a ruler if they heard you use Spanish instead of English. They wanted everyone to learn and use the English language and, over time, they succeeded to a certain degree in their desire.

I knew only the Italian I was taught at home until I entered school. The Indian child that had eroded from the wall of the Wonder Ditch would only have known its native tongue as well, a Puebloan language, or maybe even Navajo or Apache; which it had learned at home in the brush shelter or pueblo rooms of its parents.

Now that I have traveled and drifted to so many parts of the Earth like Harvard, Boulder, Australia, and Spain I can better understand the changes that took place in New Mexico throughout history, certainly since the days of the little Indian, and even those that occurred during my lifetime.

Lucien B Maxwell, for instance, the legendary rancher and land owner who created the Maxwell Land Grant that covered a large part of New Mexico, Colorado, and Arizona, was among the first settlers there. Today it is the Philmont Scout Ranch that occupies lands that were formerly owned by my father and other early settlers. This boy scout ranch is now the main focus of the area's economy and lifestyle. Each summer, as many as 20,000 boy scouts from all over the world come to watch over this part of the Earth that once only heard the voices of the American Indians and, later, the wide variety of languages of immigrant children who came from all over Europe and Mexico.

I am very happy and blessed to have lived long enough to see some of that transition. Now when I return to the town of my birth, Cimarron, I find that it is still small and quiet except when an occasional band of Harley-Davidson motorcycle riders roar through town on their way to Taos, Santa Fe or Albuquerque. Those riders don't realize that they're riding past my birthplace, the original Cimarron Opera House. I doubt also that those motorcyclists have much of an idea what happened here, or even care.

In the very early days, before I came along, it was names like Buffalo Bill Cody, Jesse James, and Annie Oakley who left there mark on the land. Now the names that are being left on the land are ones like the Charles Springer Ranch, the Chase Ranch, and those of Ted Turner and his wife, Jane Fonda.

The Federici name will also be remembered in that area for many years because my immediate family as I was growing up, as well as the new generations of Federicis, have owned stores, dance halls and movie theaters there, become lawyers and supreme court justices, and have gone into politics (and seldom lost an election—partly because they picked up the beautiful Spanish language that made them fit in easily with the local Hispanic residents of the population.

Yes, every child should have his private Wonder Ditch. I had mine, and to me it still exists as a wonderful personal spot on Earth filled with hidden treasures and memories, so much more fun and meaningful than what my grandchildren get on modern TV.

Wild Roses On A Rocky Hill

Growing up as a child in New Mexico in the early 1900's was like putting together an old-fashioned quilt. There were so many patches of colors and shapes and emotions. Any mother who has made a quilt from the outgrown school dresses and blouses and skirts and pants that once belonged to her children will tell you that long after the quilt has accomplished its purpose, all she has to do is gather the old, worn out and faded quilt to her bosom and glance at the faded geometric designs, and she can relive the days of her youth; the growing up, the challenges, the sorrows, and the days of joy, both in her life as well as her children's.

There is one pale lavender and green square of my personal quilt that reminds me of the wild roses that grew near the marker of my sister's grave in a graveyard on a rocky hill overlooking Cimarron. As a girl I remember seeing and touching those wild roses and used to wonder who had placed them there. They were identical to the wild roses I found at the water spring behind our home in Apache Hill, New Mexico.

One of the first things my father did when he arrived in this country as an immigrant was to apply for some homestead land. Much of the good land was taken, but there were a few patches in the isolated areas of Northern New Mexico. Apache Hill country was arid with no lakes or rivers, and was situated on the northern route of the Santa Fe Trail.

Our small one-room shack of discarded wood and tar paper was built in two days. A coal and wood stove with a stove pipe going up through the roof was installed and just like that we were nearly ready to go into farming and housekeeping.

The most fortunate part of that place was a spring of fresh water that trickled out of the hillside half way up the slope of Agua Dulce Mountain. An open stock tank was attached so that it could be filled continually, night and day, for stock animals of all kinds. The wild deer, coyotes and badgers, as well as our white-faced cattle appeared from everywhere early in the morning and in the late evening, and the sucking, frothy sound of their drinking could be heard all the way down to the house.

My contribution to the family in those days was to keep the large ceramic crock next to iron stove filled with fresh water from that spring. I developed sturdy little legs running up and down the path with my empty lard bucket for carrying water. I always paused at the spring for a special measure of time for myself. I had a good view from there of the surrounding country. The vastness spread before me, scratched only by a dusty roadway that lead out of the rincon to the little towns of Springer, Wagon Mound, Mora and Cimarron. I kept an eye on that dusty road because I could spot a horseman or a buggy with horses, or even a car, coming toward our house. On the rare occasion that I saw a cloud of dust rising from the road, I would rush down the hill, spilling some of the water on the way, to tell my mother that someone was coming. That would give her time to tidy up her hair and put on a clean apron and start the garlic and herbs for the pasta sauce. She would send me to a little cave that we had carved out of the hillside for a jar of apple jelly and one of the rounds of home-made cheeses that were nestled in a round wooden bowl covered with damp cheesecloth to keep it fresh and cool.

There was a flat stone that jutted out from the hillside at the spring, and one summer a bird built its nest underneath that rock. I never really saw the nest but I knew it was there because the little gray bird would rush out and startle me when I approached with my bucket and, later I could hear the chirping of the hungry young birds. Sometimes I also glimpsed a small rattlesnake at the spring, but he was very shy and would leave his favorite spot on the sunny side of the rock and slide underneath into his castle in the cool, damp world that was his kingdom.

But above all, I had my private collection of wild roses there. The dampness from the spring and the sunny exposure was just perfect for them. They were the beginning of a beautiful friendship that would last my whole life through. I would find them in later life in Australia, Italy, Connecticut, and Colorado. They would become for me like the beads of the lavender rosary that my mother presented me when I finished my catechism studies with the old priest in the mining town of Dawson.

Later on, I used to wonder at the stubbornness and tenacity of the wild roses that I found along the ancient railroad track that led to the mountains to the west of Cimarron. Sometimes my mother would send me to gather pieces of coal that had fallen off the train cars along the railroad bed. At that time, I would see the blush-pink blossoms that had pushed through the coke and ashes of the railroad beds and their bright faces smiled at me as I bent over to retrieve a shiny piece of black coal lying in the sun.

I even found roses growing along irrigation ditches when I walked through meadows picking tender dandelions for our salads in early springtime, and I found them along the hillsides and streams when I went trout fishing with my father as a girl. Patches of wild roses grew unmolested at my home in Boulder, Colorado near the fence that separated our lawn and an old neglected apple orchard.

When crushed in the palm of your hand or underfoot, wild roses smell of green apples. Yet, despite their ability to grow wild under all kinds of conditions, the blossoms will wither and drop their petals if you try to pick them and bring them indoors.

The wild roses of my life are wild and stubborn and of bittersweet fragrance, and when I come across them now, late in life, the memories that they bring set off an echo that goes on and on into eternity.

A Taste of Fear

"It's not against the law to make your own wine, Dad," Fred said, "but it is against the law to sell it." The young man sat across the breakfast table looking at his father. They were discussing a subject that I had heard my father and brother argue about ever since our family had become involved in the small business at the edge of town. It seemed that Fred and our father argued about many things. Fred was the eldest of the four children, and was the one who had to keep our father, Narciso, abreast of the way things were done in America.

In the first place, there was the language barrier. Fred and I had to explain many things to our parents concerning the running of a small business. There were licenses that had to be purchased, forms to fill out, correspondence to take care of, and income taxes and other taxes and insurance to be paid on the different properties.

The business was a combination of store, filling station and dance hall. Most of the customers came from the nearby coal-mining town of Dawson, New Mexico. In those days, most of the miners were immigrants, and the town was made up of many cultures. There were Greeks, Mexicans, Poles, Russians, Italians, quite a few English, and very few Blacks. For as long and I was old enough to remember, I had heard many languages spoken. I had been in many homes that were very different from one another and had reached the state of experience that when I helped my father deliver groceries to the homes, I knew what groceries each family would request for the next delivery even before I started writing up the orders.

The Mexicans invariably ordered lard, pinto beans, ground red chili, or ristras, which were dried chili peppers hung on long strips of twine. They also ordered small, round chilis preserved in jars, called Chili Escapeche, which was brought in from Mexico by the box-car load. They loved the cones of special brown sugar, and they always ordered a few patent medicines, such as Mexican oil, or a preparation that could be taken by mouth for stomach-ache as well as rubbed on the back or shoulders for the relief of pain.

Italians always ordered huge quantities of pasta that came in many forms: long, thin, thick, or in shapes like tubes, stars or pretzels. Since Italians ate so much pasta, I thought they must want it in different shapes in order to fool themselves into thinking they were having a varied diet. Along with the pasta, of course, they ordered olive oil in five gallon tins that were imported from Italy, and thick bitter paste made of concentrated pureed tomatoes. A can of tomato paste went a long way toward adding color, taste and thickness to the spaghetti sauce that was part of our daily diet. Pounds of dried garlic, and the cheaper cuts of beef, and homemade sausages were also a part of the Italian menu.

From the old country, each culture had also brought its special way of cooking and seasoning food. I was fascinated with the different odors lingering in the houses. The families didn't try to cover them up or air them out; maybe they didn't have any choice, since there were no air fresheners and no air-conditioning. If you could smell last night's fish in a home, it wasn't a disgrace, it was a sign that this home had had a good dinner and that the man of the house was a good provider!

The homes of the English had the least tantalizing odors to me – very bland. It seemed that most of their food was boiled. My mother never boiled any food, except minestrone, which was made with a mixture of bones, vegetables, herbs, and a little pasta.

I often wondered why there were so few French people in Dawson. I came to the conclusion that they were not the type for coal mining. The few that were there worked on the Company vegetable and fruit farm. The Blacks were segregated in an area that, at that time, was referred to as "Coon Town." I made very few deliveries there. Many Blacks couldn't afford so-called "fancy food." Also, my father wouldn't let me go into the Black area, preferring to make deliveries himself. I often wished there had been an opportunity for me to get to know that area of Dawson better. It was located at the end of a long, winding road that connected seven camps. Each camp had its own name, like Capitan or Number Seven. I never knew the types of foods my black neighbors ate, or what their homes smelled like. I've always been disappointed about that.

There was one thing that most of the people, especially those who came from Europe, had in common: they all had to have wine. Wine was always made in the home then, because in those days of prohibition there were no liquor stores. In addition, it was much cheaper to make wine yourself, and more importantly, you could make the kind that suited your own taste best.

In the early fall, my father would order several box-car loads of grapes from California. There was a special siding near the store where the train would drop off the cars at an appointed time each year. Every single grape in those cars had long before been assigned its special home up the winding, dusty road leading to Dawson. Each family would have decided early in the summer how much new wine they needed to carry them through another winter. They also had to decide how much white and how much red they would need. Most families had some of each, although "Dago-red" as it was called in those days, was by far the most popular.

I had a separate book for the grape orders. Each family had its individual account, with name, camp number, and amount of red and white grapes desired. It was a very important record book. It would have been a tragedy if some family had missed out on its quota of grapes for the year. It was either "makeup your mind how much you would need" and "put your order in on time," or do without the "lifeblood" for a whole year. Your neighbor might give you a glass now and then as a friendly, neighborly gesture, but that was all. So I guarded the order book carefully and put it into the old safe every evening.

Early in the fall, the customers would start asking, "when will the grapes be in?" On the special weekend of the delivery, the whole town took on a festive air. Cars, trucks and horse-drawn vehicles streamed down the dusty canyon to the Narciso Federici & Son General Store at Colfax to pick up the grapes. Sometimes a family had to make several trips to haul off as much as a quarter of a ton. Although I seldom helped with the box handling, I was always on hand to see that each family received its order and to keep track of the accounts.

Most of the people bought the grapes on credit, and often the wine was long gone before the bill for the grapes was paid. Sometimes the bill wasn't paid at all. However, each customer knew that it would be difficult to get grapes the next fall if the bill hadn't been paid. In some cases that I knew about, a family did without new clothes and furniture in order to pay for the grapes.

Fred and our father had many arguments about the legality of selling wine during prohibition. Narciso felt that since he was in business and since he could get grapes at wholesale price, there was no reason why he shouldn't make a few extra barrels of wine to sell here and there to needy people who couldn't afford to buy fifteen hundred pounds of grapes, and who did not have all the necessary equipment to make wine. To Narciso, selling wine just made good sense. And not only that, he would be performing an important service for his friends and customers.

The first year that Narciso made a couple of extra 50-gallon barrels of his good "Dago-red" no one particularly noticed. The children, however, were disgruntled by the fact that there were more bottles to wash, cap and store when we arrived home from school on the bus. Many times in the evenings we would have to go down into the dark, dank basement that smelled of fermenting grapes and rotting potatoes to wash bottles or transfer the wine from one barrel to another. Fred, who was then a senior in high school, started making remarks to his brothers and sisters to the effect that this was against the law. He had read in the papers that a person could make a small amount of wine for family use, but if they made more than that and, especially, if the federal agents could prove that some of it had been sold to others, the wine could be confiscated and the man of the household could be sent to jail, or fined, or both.

Since I was several years younger than my brother and since I considered him the intellectual head of the family, his words frightened me. Every time I was sent down into the basement to bring a bottle of wine upstairs to a customer, I had a feeling of dread. I feared that, at any moment, the "Federales" could come in with big silver stars on their chests and, with big guns drawn, take Dad off to prison. Most of the customers were Mexicans and English who did not make their own wine at home. They were usually my father's old friends and were happy to pay a dollar a quart. We would wrap the bottle in a paper bag, tuck it in with the groceries, and add it to the bill as "potatoes", "beans", or "apples", with a small "x" after it as our private code for our bookkeeping.

The fall that I was a sophomore in high school, there was a lot of publicity in the local papers about the raids that the federal agents were carrying out in the towns and cities of our county. Word of the raids spread quickly among the people who made their own wine. At night, after the family had gone to bed, I could hear my father talking to my mother about a raid at the Pavalitch's, or the Morganti's, or the Kazafrakis' home. The "Federales" had come to the house unannounced and gone down into the cellar and rolled the huge barrels into the street where they were broken open with axes. The beautiful red wine flowed down the hill like blood. The women gathered and held onto the children and each other as they cried. Usually, the men were away in the bowels of the mountains digging coal.

"What makes me mad is that these people were only using the wine for their own daily needs," I could hear dad's angry voice, and it sounded as though he were on the verge of tears. "Those people aren't hurting anybody, they are only doing what their fathers and grandfathers did before them. They don't get drunk and beat anybody up, and they don't rob, steal or kill. They are kind, hard-working people trying to make a living for their families and to earn enough to send their children to school, like the law says." When he talked like this, his Italian became more formal than the language he usually spoke to the family. It was as if he were making a public speech at a large gathering. My mother never said much, but I knew that she was becoming more and more anxious and concerned. Once in a while she would say, "Eh, Narciso, what would we do if they took you off to prison for several years? How would we make a living, especially now that Federico is going to law school? Povera noi!"

In my mind, the situation become enormous. I thought about it night and day, and it affected my school work. I kept thinking, suppose my father is taken to prison for being a bootlegger, how would my friends and school-mates feel toward me? They would probably laugh and make fun.

Finally, things began to seem like they were out of a detective story. There would be the rumors that the agents were sending a "spia" to buy a bottle of wine as evidence to be used against Narciso in a court of law. One had to be very careful not to sell the wine to anyone other than a trusted friend. One had to be careful who was around the store when we went into the basement and came up with the paper bag. It got so that Narciso kept his own private bottle of wine for the family table hidden in the bread box in case the agents showed up for a raid.

Finally, the war of nerves became so intense that it was decided all of the wine should be cleared out of the store and hidden elsewhere. This was no easy task when one considered that this involved moving as much as six or seven full 50-gallon barrels.

After a few days of intensive search in the nearby area, it was decided that all of the wine would be transferred to an abandoned farm about ten miles from the store. In that part of New Mexico, there were many abandoned farms; the relics of someone's dreams; someone who had homesteaded the land and hoped to make a life there only to learn, after years of trying, that this part of the country was not like Iowa and Indiana where the rains came down like God's green blessing and watered the fields and crops where all one had to do was plant and harvest.

Finally, it was decided by Narciso that the wine would be transferred to the empty farm on a particular moonless Friday night. The family waited until all of the customers had gone home and the lights were turned off. Everyone spoke in whispers and carried flashlights. The old panel truck was backed up to the entrance of the basement and several men worked feverishly to get the barrels rolled into the truck. I listened to the quiet voices and grunts of the men and the occasional curse when someone's finger got caught between two barrels. The odors of spilled wine, and of potatoes and onions and other produce that was stored in the basement, mingled with the cool, crisp fall air that came in through the open door. My job was to watch for cars on the highway that led to the store. When a car came over the crest of the hill, I would run down to the basement, and all work was suspended and all flashlights turned off until the car had climbed out of the valley.

After the barrels were loaded, the party quietly drove down a dirt road that led southeast onto the plains. The truck had to be kept in low gear, and I, following the family car, kept thinking about how much it reminded me of the many funerals we had attended in the surrounding towns where the cemeteries were desolate, dry and forsaken.

When we reached the designated farm, Narciso got out of the truck and let one of the other men drive while he directed them to the opening of an old, underground cistern. It, too, had been a part of that pioneer's dreams. Not finding water on the land, the farmer had hauled the water in to fill the cistern that was dug deep into the earth and waterproofed with concrete and covered over with timber. This cistern was now entirely dry, the wooden top was falling apart from the wind and sun, and only a few of the original planks remained. I remember thinking that it was good place for rattlesnakes.

The truck was backed into place near the edge of the cistern. The men lowered an empty barrel gently into the underground tank with ropes and Narciso climbed down with it. One end of a long garden hose was stuck into one of the barrels of wine in the truck and the other end was lowered into the cistern. The plan was for Narciso to suck the air out of the hose to create a siphon to start the flow of wine from the full barrel above into the empty barrel below.

I stood looking down into the dark cistern. The wind had turned cold, blowing down from the snowcapped mountains to the west. I wished I had put on a warmer coat. The combination of the wind and the excitement made shivers go up my back and the muscles in my legs ached. Occasionally, a coyote cut the stillness with a staccato "yip-yip" as he made his nocturnal search for food. I heard my father drawing on the hose with all his might, and gasping for breath. The hose was large, and long, and it was taking a lot of sucking to get the siphon action started.

Suddenly my father fell back and clutched his chest and throat. In the pale glow of the flashlights, I saw him make an effort to call out, but no sound came. Finally, he gestured with his hand that he was choking. I called to one of the men, then climbed down the rope, reaching for my father even before my feet touched the concrete floor. The sound of his gasping was like the rattle of death. This could not go on for long, and even in the poor light from the flashlight held by one of the men above, I could see a blue-gray look on my father's face and the white, glaring look in his eyes as he beseeched me to hit him hard on the back. I doubled up my fists and struck him on the back again and again until my arms ached and my fists felt as though they were breaking apart. Finally, a gush of red wine lashed out of his mouth and shot across the narrow enclosure of the cistern. It struck the opposite wall and a dark shadow spread like blood flowing from the neck of a chicken when you cut its neck with an ax and let it drain into the woodpile.

After a few minutes, Narciso was again able to speak and breathe normally, and the work went on into the night until all the wine had been safely transferred below ground.

I have never forgotten the fear I felt that night, watching my father struggle for his life. It was a night that could only have happened during those years of prohibition; years that will forever affect the feeling I have whenever I drink wine, even to this day.

Red Wine and Black Damp

I never lived in Dawson, New Mexico, the coal town that thrived between 1900 and 1950. But a lot of my memories and early impressions were formed there because my family had a general store and dance pavilion only six miles south of there. We called the place "Colfax."

The reason my father built his business at Colfax instead of in the town of Dawson was because Dawson was a Phelps-Dodge Corporation town, and they controlled every square inch of that canyon. Phelps-Dodge did not want competition of any kind, and they banned any kind of outside intruders. So, my father decided to build his own town with a general store, filling station, and dance and roller skating pavilion.

It was a stroke of luck that we were able to provide groceries for the residents of Dawson. Most of our business came from the miners and their families who drove to

Colfax where they were able to get many of the imported foods from Italy, Mexico and other countries. Those foods made up the daily menus in this mining community of immigrants from almost every nation in Europe as well as Mexico.

We were able to provide tons of grapes which we had shipped to Colfax from California. Those were prohibition days, and the European palate needed rich, strong, full-bodied wine with their evening meals. Every house in that community had their own homemade wine stored in their cool cellars underneath the house.

I can't remember a day or night in my parents home where there was not a pitcher of wine on the large oak dining table. It was a symbol of good living, hospitality and good health. As children, we were never forbidden to drink it as long as we poured a small amount of the dark red "juice" into a tall glass of water. Frankly, we didn't like the smell or the taste of it, and it wasn't until I was a grown, married woman that I would have a small glass with my dinner guests.

I was always amazed when they made such a fuss over my homemade wine. For my part, I preferred a cool drink of lemonade – which proves that children do not become alcoholics or drunks just because their parents drink wine in the home; it depends on the way it is served and when, usually at meal time. For all the grace of living in the atmosphere of wine in the home, I never saw anyone "in their cups" or being disrespectful or overly gregarious after a few glasses of wine.

Italians like to sing and tell a few of the off-color tales from the Old Country, especially concerning women or priests. However, there was never any profanity or four-letter words, so children could always be included in all the chatter, including during the feast-like atmosphere on holidays or weekends.

I remember how adults were pleased and looked forward to having all the children around them. It was a time to show off how good looking Federico or Anita were, and have them sing, or recite poetry. It was always a good time to show off the new baby too, − all wrapped up in cotton blankets − and try to figure out which one of the parents were reflected in that tiny, red, pinched face!

So, it was only natural that Narciso Federici's General Store supplied grapes for all those families. The way we did it was to order a railroad carload from the Napa Valley in California, sometimes directly from the Italian growers that we knew there. We placed the orders a year in advance, and the shipment always arrived at the scheduled time each year. The families drove six miles to Colfax to pick up their year's supply of grapes. Sometimes they would have to drive down to the railway siding near our business several times in order to pick up the entire order from the boxcars.

I'm always distressed when I see people throw out what is left in a glass of wine or a bottle. They have no idea what a long, tedious, and expensive process went into that glass of wine, and how many grapes it took to make even that small amount. I didn't realize it myself until I raised my own vineyard in Colorado. The small, dry sticks take so long to leaf out and flourish. In Colorado, the vines produce grapes only after five or six years; they require tending, trimming, and most of all, large quantities of water to keep the roots wet and nourished. "It takes almost as much patience and time to make a glass of homemade wine as it does to make a baby," my father used to say.

Not only were there all the different processes the liquid had to go through, but also the important part of considering the phases of the moon, so that it wouldn't turn out to be vinegar instead of wine. The first part of the long process came in the early Fall when my father prepared the barrels. These were huge 50-gallon oak barrels that he rolled out into the backyard from the cellar and filled them with water. They were open on one end, and you could see the stain of the blue-red "grapa" on the inside. He scrubbed them clean with a long-handled brush, never using soap or detergent. He left them standing full of water so the wood would become saturated, otherwise it would soak up precious grape juice later. He used a tire tool and a heavy hammer to tighten the metal straps that held the barrel together by hitting the edges toward the belly of the barrel from both ends. I remember the sounds that emanated from that procedure. It was the sound of another year passing, and the ringing sound of the promise of good wine throughout the coming year.

Our small, dark cellar had just barely enough room for six or eight standing barrels. The boxes full of the blue-black grapes were stacked along one wall. The odor of crushed grapes mingled with the odor of dry leaves, decay, and the garlands of garlic drying on the walls. The grapes were not washed but thrown by the box load into the hopper that held exactly a boxful, and the long handle was manipulated around and around, crushing everything – grapes, stems and the dark green leaves. It took several boxes of these crushed grapes, stems, leaves, and the occasional long-legged spider, to bring the load up to within a foot or two of the top of the barrel. They were punched down into each barrel with a long-handled wooded club, and then we went on to the next one.

It took several sessions of this kind of work until all the barrels were filled with the fragrant, pungent mixture. No sugar, water or other additive was incorporated into the mix. We covered each barrel with a heavy, wooden, homemade lid, and they were left to ferment. Sometimes we placed several kerosene lanterns next to the barrels to give just enough warmth to start the fermentation.

After the "action" began, we would go down into the cellar and push the mash down with the heavy club because the bubbling effect of the action tended to push the mash to the surface. As the days went by, the action slowed down until the liquid was still. Then it was time to drain the thick, dark blue liquor through a hole cut in the side of the barrel an inch or two from the bottom. This liquid was then poured into another, typically 25-gallon, barrel lying on its side. When this barrel was filled, a wooden cork was lightly placed in the hole at the top, and it was ready to go through the process of fermentation. This would take several weeks, depending on the temperature, the maturity of the grapes, and the types of grapes.

I always felt that this particular time in the wine making process was a lot like making home baked bread, or even a pregnancy. It took time, patience and wishful thinking. Every morning towards the end of this very important phase of wine-making, my father would lift the large cork at the top of the barrel lying on its side, and place his ear down to the opening to listen to hear if there was still life whispering or gurgling inside. When it became absolutely still, that was the crucial time for transferring the wine into the quart bottles that had been washed and drained and were waiting like sparkling ladies to lift their heads and become alive and filled with the dark red wine that bubbled and fizzled when first poured into them. At that time, the calendar was carefully checked to make sure that it was the right phase of the moon. If necessary, they would let the wine sleep longer – even a week or two – until the moon was right.

After the new corks were gently forced into the filled bottles, they were stacked on their sides along the wall where the boxes of fresh grapes had been stacked. During the whole process, it was the odor that impressed me the most. It was not exactly a pleasant odor, but it was fruity and decadent. Towards the end, when bottle after bottle had been filled, the fumes tended to make me light-headed, and I would have to run up the steps that led to the kitchen and walk outdoors to breathe in the fresh, clear air.

Every home in the small, mining town of Dawson was going through this experience at this time of year. The grown-ups talked about the different stages their wine-making was in. Other subjects, like sports, or gossip about neighbors, or the problems in the mines took a back seat. I often wondered if they even bothered to have sex during this period in their lives.

A coal mining town is an entity in itself. It becomes independent and almost haughty in its outlook. The experience of working in the cold, dark bowels of the earth surrounded by the dangers involved, such as cave-ins, methane gas, being run over by the coal cars, breathing in the ever-present fine black coal dust in the air that they called "the black damp." Worst of all, however, was the ever-present danger of an explosion from the coal dust in the mines. All it would take to set one off, would be a spark from a tool or piece of machinery.

In Dawson, most of the miners were Italians, but there were also Greeks, Slavs, and Mexicans. Even though they could not communicate with each other very well, there was a "pick and shovel" language that was all they needed to create a feeling of oneness and group identity. If you could hold your own with the shovel and fill your assigned cars with coal, that was all that mattered.

Coming out of the coal mines in the late evenings, sometimes in the dark of winter, carrying their water and lunch buckets, they all looked alike. The black dust covered them from top to bottom and the whites of their eyes shone like wild demons in their black faces. Many of them chewed tobacco to keep the dust from choking them. I often wondered how they could possibly ever get clean again. Their wives must have spent most of their time washing their clothes for the next day's work. You could always recognize a coal miner, even in his best Sunday clothes. Somehow, the dust clung to their eyelashes and under their fingernails. It hung on to them like a permanent masquerade.

It was no wonder that on Saturday nights they would all gather at the local company bar and pool hall. There were no women there; so different from the bars of today. Those few hours of drinking and companionship among their own kind was all they had to look forward to during the whole week. There is no doubt that they sometimes overdrank, trying to forget the week that was coming toward them, day after tomorrow, like a loaded locomotive full of fear and dread. Which one of them would be the next to have a rock crush them to death, or a leg or arm torn off by the coal cars. Or, God forbid, that flash of light, that black thunder, and then darkness with the weight of a whole mountain on top of your chest.

Is it any wonder that when the bar finally closed and they walked in the darkness to their own small wooden homes, sometimes, the sound of cries from the women and even the children, floated into the still, early morning air. The pain and degradation that some men had to go through in order to pay for the bread of life and the caring of their children was a monstrous thing to see.

On Sundays in church I sometimes noticed the sad, pinched faces of the women, wearing black shawls over their heads. More than once, when a shawl fell back from a woman's face as they knelt during Mass, I got a glimpse of a swollen eye or lip, and some kind of discoloration. And yet, even so, there was evidence of love. That man loved his wife and children as he knelt with them in prayer, and walked with them to the altar to receive communion, you could see the sadness and need of forgiveness on his face, even in the way he walked. Here was a creature doing penance, and as he fingered the beads of the rosary, he was truly sorry and repentant, and his family knew and forgave him.

I found myself a part of this life; yet I was one of the lucky ones – my father and brothers didn't have to lead the life of a miner. My family had chosen to live and work near the mines and the miners, but not to become a part of their profession and culture.

We delivered groceries into all of their homes and I got to glimpse a considerable part of their lives, but I still felt apart from them. I admired them, and learned to speak their languages so that I could better serve them with the groceries they needed. I sometimes watched and helped with a new birth, surrounded by some of the neighborhood women. Sometimes the midwife did not speak the language of the suffering new mother, but birth has an international language of its own. We are all born, more or less, in the same fashion, with the same pains and concerns. That very fact would bombard my brain years later when I had a husband and, later a son, in two different wars. I would tell myself that if the women could rule, there would never be wars. You cannot destroy anything that you have created on your own. That dream, that plan, that creative urge within a woman, and all the struggle and pain, and conflict and passion she has endured would never let her tolerate a living creature to be dismissed, forgotten, or made to suffer.

As a teenager, I had the normal urges that come as part of that phase in one's life. Although I was not allowed to go out on dates, I was around and near the young men and women of this isolated town in the American West, I attended classes in school with all of them, I noticed the beautiful curly black hair and clear wonderful eyes and the young, strong bodies. Some of them had beautiful voices and loved to sing with me. In later years, when I heard or saw Frank Sinatra, I felt a homesickness and yearning to be back in that place and time where a young man's voice could tempt me to forget all of my future dreams. Some of us had come from the same clay from the other side of the world. Our parents spoke the same language and attended the same church, and even ate the same food. And yet, deep in my heart, I could not see myself growing up in the shadow of this coal-filled mountain. My dreams were different, and I knew I could not be happy growing up to watch my husband come out of the depths of this mountain, covered with black coal dust, and reach for me at the end of the day with his passion, and with his frustration for needing and wanting something more.

During many of the classes I attended with the young, beautiful people, I saw the talent that was wasted. I could see famous actors, musicians, artists, and singers beneath the surface of these children. They had sensitive, creative minds, with a love for life and beauty and a need to accomplish something that would live long after they were gone. To me, it was a sin and a heartless thing to see them follow their fathers into that black hole: to live through it, if they were lucky, if not, to die of black lung – coughing and spitting and sitting in the shadows of their wooden houses while waiting for a miserable death; or worse still, to be one of the many they would carry out after an explosion.

I couldn't see myself waiting at one of the portals of the mines, surrounded by children and all the other wailing mothers and wives. Too many times I had seen it happen and endured the many wakes at the homes where the bodies lay in their cheap, wooden coffins surrounded by cheap, homemade paper flowers and bits of embroidery. I often thought in my young mind that sorrow and compassion was lost on these poor widows.

They would survive and find another life; but the beautiful, unfulfilled lives in those coffins would never feel the warmth of sunshine or flakes of snow melting on their beautiful foreheads. They would never again come to life at the sound of the beautiful music from the bands that played every Saturday night at my father's dance hall, the Colfax Pavilion. What a waste and what a crime. I knew that I would walk away from it all someday and although I would never forget it, I knew that I had to find something else out there in the big, beautiful world of America and all its opportunities.

I'm thankful for having experienced Colfax Pavilion. It was a place and a time that will never return again. What made it so special was all the different people who gathered there from all over the world. It was a bright, beautiful and happy place full of big band music, where from the first strain of horns, banjos, drums and piano, the world became a magic place. Life became worthwhile, and all the sadness and pain and struggle was lost in the beautiful sway of the music and there wasn't an awkward sound or action among the hundred or more couples who held each other tenderly and drifted into a Never-Never-Land that they would remember to their dying day.

*Ann's mother, Divina, at left, with her sister, Marietta, in the doorway of the
house in Prota, Italy where Divina was born. The caption reads "Marietta e
Divina sula porta della casa dove sono natti en Prota Italia. Julio - 1950."*

A portrait taken in Cimarron in 1915. From left to right: Sister Benecia, who tragically died as a child after falling from a tricycle, Narciso, Fred, Divina, and Ann.

At the Opera House, on the left are Narciso, Divina, Bill, Ann, and Fred. In the center is Narciso's brother, Guido, his wife, Julia, and daughters Mary, Enis, and Lilly. At right are Ernesto and Marietta with children Edith and Federico.

A studio portrait of the Federici children taken in about 1924-1925. Ann is on the right, brothers Fred and Bill on the left, and sister Emma on the pedestal.

Sketch of the adobe hut that served as Narciso and Divina's first home in Cimarron, complete with sunflowers growing on the earthen roof.

Narciso and Divina's house (the "G & G House") in Cimarron in the old days. The caption on the back reads "Home. July '43". Grandchildren Mike and Margie Rosso still live there, where they raised another Divina; a great-grandchild.

The Opera House in Cimarron, New Mexico, built by Ann's father, Narciso. The family living quarters were on the ground floor, at right, and movies and dances took place upstairs. The author performed "Little Miss Muffet" there when she was three. Divina, on left, with two Mexican women who worked for her.

The inscription reads, "Ann Federici, 12 years old. Taken in Dawson, N. Mexico by photographer John Caraglio."

The author in an unusually playful pose.
Taken in Cimarron Canyon by sister,
Emma.

Ann in the back seat of a car.
She appears to be enjoying a beverage.

One of a number of "pin-up" photos of the
author taken at the request of Curtis when
he was overseas in The War. Taken by
her sister, Emma, in the back yard of the
Cimarron house in the 1940s.

Ann, showing off her beautiful long hair
and new dress. In the back yard of the
Cimarron house in the 1940s, taken by
Emma.

Curtis and Ann in the 1930s. The photo frame is embossed with the name "Williston Studio".

Curtis, looking dapper as usual. Maxwell, New Mexico, April 1940

A sad event for Ann and Curtis. The souvenir photo frame from Eddie's Nite Club Photos, is inscribed "San Francisco -- just before Curtis left for the Pacific. 1943."

*Narciso and Divina in the back yard of the "G & G House"
in Cimarron in 1956.*

*Ann's parents, Narciso and Divina, in Cimarron. The photo was taken by
Ann's son, Curtis in the early 1970s. He always wore that hat outside and
she always wore her head scarf, indoors and out.*

The author, at right, with brother Fred and his first wife, Ann. Caption reads *"Taken on Raton Pass the day we went to Trinidad."* Ann (the author) remembers that *"someone was going to get some dental work done."*

Ann's brother, Fred and his second wife, Ruth. Taken in front of the author's house in Boulder in 1964, shortly before Ann, Curtis, and the boys moved to Australia for a year. It was the last time the family saw Fred, as he died of cancer while they were away.

Ann's sister, Emma, probably in Cimarron. The handwritten caption on the back reads simply: "Five by Five", July '43.

The author's sister, Emma, and her husband Lawrence "Lento" Rosso, at their home in Cimarron on Christmas, 1985.

Ann's brother, Bill, and his wife, Elsie. Taken in the 1940s.

Ann's son, Brooke at the author's house on 10th Street in Boulder.
Apparently, a photographer was going door to door with his pony soliciting
portraits.

Taken by Boulder Daily Camera photographer.
It ran in the paper on Christmas Eve, 1954.
The caption read: "Little children, Brooke
and Curt Martin, and dog Tippy, watch with
childish wonderment and happy hopes for the
jolly man in the red coat who brings happiness
to all in the Night before Christmas."

A baby picture of Brooke and Curt taken at the
first Boulder house, on 10th Street, in 1950.

A formal portrait of the Martin family. Taken in Boulder in approximately 1960.

A portrait of the Martin family in Boulder in 1952.

The author's husband, Curtis, with sons, Brooke and Curt, pheasant hunting between Boulder and Longmont, Colorado in the late 1950s. A housing development and shopping center now stand at this location.

"Two Guns Against the Republicans Are Better Than One"

Designate

CURTIS MARTIN

For

UNITED STATES SENATE

♦ Expert on Problems of War and Peace

♦ Author: "Colorado Politics"

9

CURTIS MARTIN
2018 HERMOSA DR., BOULDER

Curtis' calling card during his bid for the US Senate. His campaign slogan was "Two Guns Against the Republicans Are Better Than One."

Ann's son, Brooke, and his wife
Lucy, celebrating their 35th wedding
anniversary in Hawaii in 2008.

The author's youngest son, Curtis
William, and his wife, Marsha Kosteva.
Taken in San Francisco by photographer,
Jim Sugar, in about 1995.

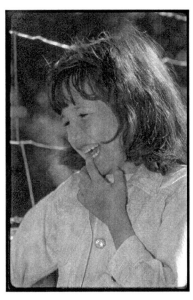

Ann's grandson, Dylan (Brooke and
Lucy's son), in his senior photo from
Santa Fe High School in 1996.

The author's granddaughter, Hilary
(Brooke and Lucy's daughter). Taken in
Flora Vista, New Mexico in 1990.

A formal portrait of the author. Written on the face of the photo, she has inscribed, "Love, Dadums," one of Curtis' nicknames for her.

The author bundled up in a hooded, fur coat. Taken in Boulder in the 1970s.

A photo of Ann in the backyard of the family home in Boulder. Taken in the 1970s.

The author taking a speed boat ride on Navajo Reservoir near Aztec, New Mexico. A large family reunion took place on a house boat there in 1989 in celebration of the 40th birthdays of Ann's son, Curtis, and her nephew, Richard.

A Federici family reunion in Santa Fe in 1985 at the home of Ann's brother, Bill. The author is in the back row, third from left, and husband, Curtis is to the right of center wearing a white jacket.

A reunion of Federicis, Rossos, and Martins in Emma and Lento's back yard in Cimarron in 1992. Despite the happy faces, it was a somber event; the funeral of Ann's husband Curtis. Ann is in the center wearing a black and red sweater.

A ceramic sculpture by Ann entitled "The Etruscan Lady".

One of many sculptures that Ann created during her years in Boulder and Flora Vista, New Mexico. She worked in wood, stone, and bronze.

I'm Forever Blowing Bubbles

The dances that my father hosted in the Opera House gave me some insight into the variations of dancing from different cultures—from beautiful Spanish waltzes to the Varsuviana, to the Rancheras, etc. I consider myself fortunate that I, growing up in the American Southwest, was able to hear the music and songs, and watch the dances from other cultures, for it was in them that I was provided with a glimpse into the myths, legends and folk tradition of the Indians, Spanish and Mexicans which now make up the Chicano Culture.

I remember a woman, Mrs. Jose Maldonado, who told me much about her background. She was born in the State of Michoacan, in Mexico, and she used to tell me about the beauty of its countryside, the charm of its people, and their exquisite songs. She married a Spaniard and they came up from Mexico on a flat-car on the railroad to work in the coal mines of Northern New Mexico. That union eventually produced eight or nine children.

She once told me that after the Conquest, the Tarascans learned religious music from the Catholic friars and started to use stringed instruments such as the guitar and fiddle. She said that the pulsating music of the Negroes of the Gulf Coast also became part of the musical language of the Michoacan. She told me that they sang pirecuas; what she felt were the most romantic songs in all Mexico. She said that in the mestizo areas there was wide use of instruments like the arpa grande, vihuelas, jaranas, and guitars.

As they lived out in the country in considerable isolation they were out of touch with town and city life and depended on music and dance for their entertainment and social life. They took great pride in their musicianship and creative abilities and made up new songs for every event that happened whether it was a murder or a marriage. Folk music was a very important part of their Indian life.

Since they were country folk, many of their songs and dances, Mrs. Maldonado said, had to do with the birds and even the snakes. In the dances called Jalisco the young dancer strikes at an imaginary snake with his hat. There were other dances where the dancers act like courting doves. Two songs that she used to sing that I enjoyed so much were Flor de Canela and Malva Rosita.

In my experience then, I can only say that the differences between these Indian songs and dances and the ones I heard and experienced in New Mexico were in the rhythm and in the song content. The Indian songs and dances seemed more primitive to me and I guess I will never really know since Mrs. Maldonado said that the ancient Tarascan music, a fine art, was stilled forever because the Mexican civilization of that time was fast disappearing never to be the same again.

Living in that western town of Cimarron, in Northern New Mexico, I also was in the midst of a great change and a great mixture of cultures. Since my father had a public business of entertainment which included theater, athletic hall, as well as dance hall, I was able to witness this cultural melting pot first hand.

I was surrounded by Indians, Mexicans, Spaniards, cowboys, ranchers, coal miners, stonemasons, and gold miners and I could see and hear how each influenced the other. For instance, my father's Italian name was Narciso Federici. Few in America could pronounce it, so, adopting the practice of the many immigration officials to list his last name first, he began to introduce himself as Fred Narciso, a name much easier for English-speakers to pronounce and remember.

Usually I found that music and dance mixed and, in my part of the world, was influenced primarily by the Mexican and Spanish because of the large numbers of them in the area. The Anglos were in the minority so their music and dance, and even language, were influenced more than the other way around. It wasn't long until the cowboy learned the Varsovillana or the Ranchera and he picked up some of the verses of the songs he heard every day, especially the love songs. "Querida" and "Amor" and "Beso" came before "Comida" and "frijole" and "chili," but it wasn't long until many other words and customs were picked up. For instance, the cowboy learned right away to "roll your own" cigarette from the Mexicans sitting on the corner. He learned to wear a bright kerchief around his neck or across his forehead. He had never done that before.

It wasn't long until every home had a "mano" and "metate"—stone grinding tools—to use for grinding corn. Certainly this came from the Indian whether that Indian came from Mexico or Taos Pueblo. The women started wearing "squaw skirts" as they were called in those days. They were practical skirts because you could squat and stoop over without showing your drawers and the women in those days had to do a lot of squatting and stooping!

Of course, cultural influences traveled both ways, and I noticed that the Mexican girls and Spanish girls had started cutting off her lovely braids and using lipstick and cheek-color. Some of them started smoking cigarettes and skipping church service, especially Confession. It wasn't long until they were using phrases like "Hi, Jonny" or "Hi, Cowboy" and singing a song that was then popular in English, entitled, "I Want a Rubber Dolly" or "I'm Forever Blowing Bubbles"!

In other words, the most important influences in the folk music and dance were brought about by what the Majority, in this case the Spanish-speaking cultures, happened to be doing as their thing. Certainly the Italians had very little influence in that setting because there weren't enough of them. We could sing "0 Solo Mio" all day and no one would pick that up because there weren't enough of us. So we ended up learning to sing Chicano songs, dance their dances, and eat their kind of cooking, and you will find it so even today in that part of the country. Even the "Southwest Style" house I built in Boulder has been influenced by the Indian and the Spanish so, you see, it sticks once it gets into the blood.

Dance, music, as well as Folk Art, is what makes up LIFE. It makes up the life and history of the people who created it and brought it together. For me the songs I had learned, and the words of those songs, told me more about these people than the dances.

I will never forget the first time I saw the Pueblo Indian dancers in Taos when I was a little girl. I couldn't understand why the women seldom danced and why the Indian had to use rattles and drums instead of violins and guitars, and why they were half-naked when they danced. I didn't realize at the time that when they danced, they were dancing to please their gods. They danced so that they could have rain for their corn, beans, and squash, or to have good luck in hunting, or for success in a battle.

I watched the polka being danced at the Saturday night dances in the old Opera House. My mother, Divina, told me that she danced it in her little town in Northern Italy before she came to this country. She and Dad were so pleased to see that the Mexicans and Spanish also danced the polka. It made her feel that there was not that much difference in their culture if they could do the same dances even though they could not understand each others' languages.

The Magic of Music

Even though I grew up in a small community in Northern New Mexico, I never heard the word mestizo used back then. The village was a mixture of Mexican, Spanish, and Indian, and I, as an Italian, was the outsider: at home only Italian was spoken, and it wasn't until I entered school that I learned English. In that regard, I experienced the same thing as all of my playmates who spoke Spanish in their homes and didn't learn English until they too had reached school age. In order to fit in with them, enjoy their games, and adapt to their ways, I learned Spanish "in the street," and I learned it quickly not only because of my need, but also because it was very much like Italian.

What does this all have to do with Music?

Most of the things I learned about my Chicano friends and neighbors came through learning and listening to their music. I learned how they felt about religion, about the family, quite a bit about their history, about the things they had suffered in life as well as the things they had enjoyed. I heard about their lives in Mexico as well as their homes in Spain, and I heard some of the songs by the Indians about their worship of the sun and mountains. All of this blended into a culture that I had no name for: it wasn't Mexican or Spanish or Indian. They were all simply "friends," "neighbors", "school chums." Certainly at that time there was no such word as Chicano or mestizo. At least, I never heard them used.

The only thing that they seemed to have in common, as far as I was concerned, was the language. They certainly didn't all look alike. Some were very dark with black eyes and black hair. Some were white-skinned and blue eyed, with light brown hair. Their nose profiles or cheek bones were not alike. Some were taller than others and some were quite small and slender in proportion.

Of course they all attended the Catholic Church, as did I. I remember marveling to myself how all these people from so many different cultures and so many different parts of the earth, all went to the same church.

Again, what does this have to do with Music?

The music in that church was the same for all of us, and even though they sang some additional hymns besides the music of the Mass, I could always understand those hymns even when they were sung in Spanish because they were almost the same in Italian.

So you can see that Music brought us together in many ways.

I remember a lecture in one of my classes about the "Music of the Mestizo." It was mostly new to me although I grew up and lived with people who must have been "half-breeds" of one culture or another. I had to look up the meaning of "Mestizo" in my Spanish dictionary to know that it meant the mixture of two or more cultures. Does that necessarily mean that the music I heard as a child was Mestizo Music? I don't think so.

One thing I know for certain was that I loved the music of these people who were Spanish-speaking. I had no idea whether they were Oratorios or Coplas or Decimas or Corridos. What I liked best about the songs and the way they were sung was the blending of the voices. The harmony was always there and it remained with you long after the song was over. It could be a song about love, about the home they left in Mexico or Spain, or about the Indian reservation. Most of it was sad music and I always wondered about that as a girl—why was it always so sad?

There were only three Italian families in Cimarron when I was growing up. They too had their own music; however about the only time I ever heard them sing much was after they had had too much home-made wine. The Italians songs were often taken from the Operas they had seen and heard in Italy, or they were humorous songs about the fat lady or the man who wanted to go out with somebody else's woman! Then, there were always songs like "0 Sole Mio," but that song was not really about love, or history, or sadness, as it might seem. It was just a song about how beautiful it is to have a day of sun after a storm. However, Dad did have one song of protest he used to sing quite a bit about "Il General Cadorna." It was a song about the difference between the General in the Italian Army and the foot soldier. In it, the words tell about how the General ate steaks while the foot soldiers ate only dried chestnuts! No wonder Dad came to America to escape the draft into the Italian Army!

One day, during my trip to Europe with my husband, Curtis, I was waiting for a bus in Toledo, Spain. Three little girls were skipping down a steep, stone-cobbled street on their way home from school and they were singing, "Adelita." I had learned to sing that very same song many years before, as I was growing up in a little village clear across the world from Toledo. When I was in Mexico years later and they sang it in their Folklorico Opera, I was told that it was a song that had originated with Pancho Villa and his followers. How could a song like that criss-cross the whole earth and all these different cultures and find a home in my heart too? I guess it is partly the magic of Music.

In Cimarron, I had had two families as neighbors, one on either side of my house. Their names were Maldonado and Chavez. They both spoke Spanish but they sang different songs and ate different foods cooked in totally different ways. Their faces and hair were different, different color, different profiles. I liked them both but they didn't seem to like each other too well. I never knew why. I thought they had so much in common; their language, their church, they both worked on ranches nearby.

Mrs. Chavez taught me songs like Don Simon, El Vueyecito Canelo, La Indita, El Asturiano, and El Testamento.

Mrs. Maldonado told me she had come from a place in Mexico in the State of Michoacan. Her songs were quite different and sometimes I could not quite understand the words. One was entitled La Visita, Flor de Canela, Una Noche Serena i Oscura, etc. When Mrs. Maldonado came to our little country store, she asked for blanquillos instead of huevos, plátanos instead of bananas, etc.

It was the Music that made it easy to get to know and understand my neighbors in that little town.

So, naturally, it was with great interest that in later years I was to come across a collection of songs by another Chavez, this one being Alex Chavez. He was our neighbor for some time in Boulder and I found that he was also singing "El Testamento" and "Julia Mia," etc., the songs I had heard in Cimarron as a child. I asked Mr. Chavez about these songs and he said that most of the songs he sang came out of his own experience, from his own people. He had learned them from within his family circle in the San Luis Valley in southern Colorado, where he had grown up. The folk ways of the Spanish in the entirety of Mexico, Central and South America, and the American Southwest is rich in song. Years later, I was given a record that had been recorded in the state of Michoacan in Mexico by Henrietta Yurchenco. Here again, I was pleasantly surprised to hear some of the songs that Mrs. Maldonado had sung to me when I was just a girl in New Mexico.

Miss Yurchenco had recorded the music as part of her research in Mexico in 1942, in the State of Michoacan, where a rich folk-culture abounds. She says that early in the 16th century, in Tzintzuntzan, capital of the Tarascan

Empire, the Conquistadores were treated to an evening's entertainment of songs and dances which, according to the Spanish chroniclers, were "sad enough to have risen from hell." It was hardly a time for rejoicing, for the death knell of Mexican civilization was already sounding. It wasn't long until the ancient Tarascan music, a fine art, was stilled forever. Yurchenco says that after the Conquest, the Tarascans learned religious music from the Catholic friars and became acquainted with stringed instruments such as the guitar and fiddle and learned some of the songs brought by the Conquerors. Within a few decades, both Tarascans and "mestizos" had developed their own indigenous musical expression. The Indians of Lake Patzcuaro sang their pirecuas, some of the most romantic songs in all Mexico. Highland Indians also sang abajenos. In "mestizo" areas there was a lively, explosive music for such stringed instruments as the arpa grande, vihuelas, jaranas, and guitars and best of all the lyrics were pungent!

Mostly, what interested me is the fact that Mrs. Maldonado was singing to me songs like La Visita, El Son Del Viento, Fulanita, Magnolia, Flor De Canela and all the time, I didn't know that these were "mestizo songs", a combination of Mexican and Indian folk music and that they were composed and exchanged when work was done, during work-bees when the Highland and Lake Indians helped each other with the harvest, on Saints' days, or for the dawn serenades. These Tarascans were out of touch with town and city life and music was very, very vital and they were proud of their musicianship and creative abilities.

I am thankful that I was touched in a small way by all these cultures, especially through their Music!

Spanish Folklore in My Youth

My parents were of Italian heritage and spoke very little English at that time but they quickly learned Spanish because it was spoken by the majority of the people that we lived and worked with. My playmates were almost all Chicanos as well as my schoolmates and we only learned English when we attended the public school there.

As a result of this, I was to hear much Chicano music, especially since my father owned and operated what they called "La Opera." It was a two-story, large stone building which he had built with the help of two or three Chicano stone-masons. I was born in that building as the living quarters were on the first floor. Today the building still stands and is being used as a Methodist Church.

All community activities took place at "La Opera" at that time. We had traveling shows known as Chautauqua Shows which included Shakespearian plays, comedies, farces, mimes, public-speaking, strong-man acts, magic shows, and dance groups.

However, on Saturday nights my father held public dances. Every other Saturday night was turned over to the Chicanos. Their music consisted of violin, guitar and arpa grande or the big standing harp. The refreshments which came at midnight consisted of hot coffee and tamales made by the tomalero who walked across town with his huge enameled bucket filled with the fragrant, husk-covered treats. Even as a little girl, I would have permission to stay up until the tomalero came at midnight so that I could have one of his fantastic creations!

The Anglos had their night of public dances on the other Saturday nights. Their orchestra consisted of piano, drums, banjo and saxophone and their refreshments would typically be small, dainty sandwiches made earlier during the day and wrapped in white, soft napkins, white or chocolate cake, and coffee.

As a result, I grew up listening to Chicano music as well as the jazz of that era played by the Anglos. I preferred the Chicano music because it was more colorful and active, and the rhythm of the waltzes, shotis, polkas, and special group dances like La Varsuvianana, and La Raspa captured my imagination as a child.

Singing was a family as well as community experience in those days before radio and TV; the family often sang together around the fireplace or pot-belly stove in the evenings. The singers took pride singing in harmony and usually someone accompanied them with a piano or guitar. In addition to the social singing there was the singing that was part of church services with hymns from Spain and Mexico. Also I was able to hear much of the singing that took place at the velorios, the celebration of the dead, which took place during wakes, in the homes of the relatives.

The Chicano songs that I heard in those days were a mixture of songs from Spain and Mexico and a few that had originated in northern New Mexico and Southern Colorado. Not only did these songs introduce me to the Spanish language, but they also interpreted for me much of the culture and folklore of these people. I could always learn something new or strange about a culture if it was introduced to me in the form at music. I have always felt that the best way to teach children a language, and the folklore of an area or culture, is to teach them the local songs, particularly those that have been handed down by past generations.

Eventually I grew up, married, and left the little town of Cimarron, and after much travel, settled down in Boulder, Colorado. It was at that time that I was fortunate to meet Mr. Alex Chavez. He too had been born and raised in the American Southwest near a small town in the San Luis Valley called Capulin. Alex played the guitar beautifully and it wasn't long until he and his family joined us for evenings of singing in our home in Boulder. The little villages of Cimarron and Capulin came together in song in that Colorado college town, and we soon discovered that the songs which arose from the folklore of the areas where we had grown up had a great deal in common.

We compiled notes and found that some of the songs we knew overlapped, and even though there were some minor differences in the lyrics, the origin and content regarding Spanish folklore, was much the same since we had both grown up in an area where a lot of people from Spain had settled down many years before.

We found that many of the songs expressed the realistic, humorous, tragic, and romantic attitudes that the Spanish-speaking people had inherited from Spain and Mexico, as well as the traditions and the folklore of the American Southwest.

Two of the songs I learned from Alex that I was sure had come out of his own experience in the San Luis Valley were La Viejita y los Animales, a comical and lighthearted song about an old woman who took all her farm animals to bed with her at night, and the other was titled "Julia Mia," a very tender love song.

Many of the other songs like El Testamento had come from Old Spain with the early settlers to this raw new world in New Mexico and Colorado. In this song, the man asks a scribe or scrivano to record his earthly possessions; items like a nice big ham, or an old shirt, or a hat made of rabbit fur.

One song we used to sing was entitled La Indita. This song has as its setting an Indian Pueblo near Santa Fe named Cochiti. It is a love song being sung to a little Indian maiden. Certainly this song wasn't brought from Spain or Mexico but originated in that area of New Mexico. After all, the Spanish and the Indian had been living in the same area for a long time and it was natural that this kind of song would sooner or later spring to life.

Another song was El Pavo Real, The Peacock. It is
said that this song originated in Mexico. To me, this song
seemed to be a sad song of homesickness of someone who
had come to New Mexico from Old Mexico and missed his
homeland and his loved ones very much. For me, this song
seems to have some of the Mayan symbols like the Royal
Peacock and Rays of Gold.

"Pavo real que eres correo
Y te vas al rayar del oro
Si te preguntan que hago
Pavo real diles que lloro
Lagrimitas de me sangre
Por un Amor que yo adoro..."

Another song, Tecolotito has evidence of New Mexican
Indian in it. In this song the Tecolotito or little owl has
flown from his Indian pueblo to a strange place. In the song
the singer asks:

"Tecolotito de donde vienes
Vengo del pueblo colorido..."

and goes on to say...

"Si los muchachos tuvieran
La libertad del coyote..."

In other words, pueblo colorido and coyote are most
definitely New Mexican, or at least of the Southwestern
United States.

On the other hand, the song El Asturiano apparently
came from Spain and is usually sung at weddings. The song
helps you see, in your mind's eye, the handsome Asturian

man – a sort of Dandy – with his fancy clothes, a pointed hat, and a lovely cane. The song intimates that he dresses well but works very little! The lyrics go on into wedding folklore to say:

"En la puerta de esta casa
'Sta una paloma parada
Entrará con su marido
Si le permiten l'entrada..."

This verse strikes me as filled with images of Spanish folklore regarding virginity and the chorus of the song goes on to express in beautiful lyrics that the best man and the bridesmaid will soon wash their hands in that symbolic river that runs in its crystalline, virgin and untarnished form which embodies for me, the marriage ceremony and all that it must have meant to those people in those days. The reference to the little dove waiting to enter the door with her husband and the crystalline waters that will never again be as clear and fresh and clean again is filled with meaning and symbolism for me.

For me, it is folk songs like these that help preserve the music, language, and cultural heritage of today's Chicano. We owe a debt of gratitude to those who continued to sing those songs, and play and dance to that music; people like Alex Chavez. It is sad for me to think how many children, as well as adults, of Spanish and Mexican ancestry have missed out on these songs simply because they are no longer performed in the evenings after dinner, as they had been in the old days.

Return to Montecito

I had no idea I would ever return to Montecito. A World War and a husband in the Pacific changed all that.

The bright, sunny morning in San Francisco, while we were waiting for two separate taxis to take us on our separate ways after we had been married for over ten years was like a stroke of lightning. Things would never be the same after that. It would change our lives completely, and we wouldn't be the same people by the time we were reunited in that same city four years later.

We had practically grown up together as children in that small town in New Mexico. We knew each other's friends and families. It wasn't until we finished high school that we realized we were attracted to each other. Curtis was always one of the top students and an excellent runner in track. We only had one class together during that time, and that was Spanish. Having learned Spanish from my childhood playmates, the class was dull for me and I stopped raising my hand when the teacher asked questions because it became embarrassing for me to know all the answers. Sometimes, I came in early in order to help the teacher, Mr. Mollard, prepare for the day's lesson. In those days, teachers had to instruct several subjects and sometimes they found themselves teaching classes they weren't prepared for; subjects they had not had the right schooling for in college. Many of the subjects the teachers could fake, but not the foreign languages. The students caught on right away and the class would deteriorate into small jokes and smart aleck remarks by the students. This must have been very trying for a young schoolteacher teaching a strange class in a small western town. That's why I was happy when I could help Mr. Mollard. Perhaps Curtis, as a fellow student, noticed that, and it might have been the beginning of his admiration for the little Italian girl with the long light brown braids down her back.

Later, Curtis would go on to college, but I remained at home in the tradition of Italian immigrant girls. My two brothers would attend law schools but I stayed at home learning the skills of being a wife, mother and builder of a family for some proper spouse.

When Curtis came home from school on holidays or long weekends, he was drawn to me and the Colfax Pavilion which I helped manage for my father and mother. The Pavilion was twelve miles from Curtis' home but he was always there when the first strains of the big bands began to play. It seemed like a natural thing. We both loved to dance and we made a striking couple with my long flowing hair and his blond curly mass all over the top of his head. From the beginning, they started calling us "the lovers," partly because we never danced with any of the other young people. Eventually, the young men from the neighboring towns who attended the dances didn't even bother to ask me for a dance. They seemed to know I was "spoken for."

Sometimes Curtis would come over on Sundays, too, before leaving on the long drive to the university in Albuquerque. My parents and siblings soon accepted him as part of the family, and he would sit down at the table with us and seemed to relish my mother's Italian dishes. But, it was my father that caught Curtis' eye and heart. My father, Narciso, liked to ask him about his classes at the college and when he discovered that Curtis liked to hear his stories about the Old Country, he became like a man enchanted, with an audience that he had longed for all his life.

Curtis listened attentively because these stories were so different from the ones his own dad must have told him. His father was Pennsylvania Dutch and he didn't talk very much; when he did it was mostly about sports. Dad, on the other hand, was so pleased to finally have someone who listened and laughed at his stories that sometimes he embellished them to make them better than they actually were and my mother would have to interject in Italian, to tell him to "calm it down" and stick more closely to the truth. But my father was a storyteller and nothing could restrain him once he started on a good tale. His English was spiced with Italian – but that made it even more entertaining for Curtis. Years later when Curtis repeated those stories or wrote about them in his books, he always had them down in the colorful way that he had heard them, in that way we were able to enjoy them all over again long after my father was gone.

While Curtis was in school we wrote letters faithfully to each other and by the time I finished high school, I knew there would be only one man for me; for life. I lost interest in all the other young men I encountered at the Pavilion. Somehow, the miners, farmers, ranchers and cowboys had become like creatures from another planet. I only waited for the letters and the meetings with Curtis.

At one Christmas dance, after I finished high school in Dawson, Curtis asked me to marry him in September of the following year. When we asked my parents, the first thing they wanted to know was how was he going to make a living. They made it clear that they wanted us to wait. Yet, as September approached, we decided to go ahead with our wedding plans. However, it would have to be kept a secret. We spoke to my brother, Fred, then an Assistant District Attorney in Taos, and his wife Ann, regarding the proposal. They admired Curtis so much, and could see the potential in him, so they agreed to have us come to their home on a weekend in early September and we arranged a simple wedding ceremony.

All of us have certain chapters made up of magic moments in our lives. Certainly, that September day in Taos, New Mexico with the autumn colors, the odors of burning piñon wood, and the colorful mixture of Spanish, Mexican and Indian people intermingling with the surge of youth and love, were woven into a blanket that we were wrapped up in for the rest of our lives together. We kept that wedding a secret from our parents and, even after we were married again, publicly, years later, we never told them.

It wasn't long after Curtis left for duty in the South Pacific that Dad and I looked around the small, comfortable home in Cimarron and decided we had to have a project of some kind to take our minds off the war, and how much I missed my husband. Dad was too old by then to cut stone or build houses, so we both came upon the idea of Montecito Ranch, situated twenty-five miles away. It was sitting there with only an old couple living in the ranch house, rent free. There were no cattle on the place and it suddenly dawned on us that there were 2500 acres of idle grazing land including several windmills pumping water into unused water tanks. Why not start building a herd of white-faced cattle?

We had raised cattle there before, but when Dad retired and the children left, he discontinued his trips to the ranch with the exception of going down two or three times a year to check the fences. He found that some of the neighbors were coming in at night and lifting up the bottom strand of the barbed wire fence to let in flocks of sheep to graze at night and then herding them back to the home place and lowering the strand of barbed wire. We could always tell where it had happened because we would find tufts of wool on the barbs where they had caught on the backs of the larger animals.

We didn't really mind because we weren't using the grazing land at this time, but after we started our herd of cattle we decided that we would have to discourage the practice. Dad would say in Italian, "It's like having a neighbor lady or wet nurse feed your children." Wet nursing was a common practice in the Old Country, he said, because the women of wealth didn't want to spend the time it takes to nurse a child several times a day. He said that a good wet nurse was hard to find. Many times they would bring them into the home to live with them until the child was "breast broken." Sometimes, if the wet nurse needed money to supplement the family income, she would stay on and the child would have his or her own supply of good rich "mother's" milk until he was three or four years old.

Narciso claimed that some of the top scholars and philosophers, business men and artists were raised with wet nurses. They became solid, leading citizens because there had been no stress in their early years. They realized who their natural mothers were, but they always had a fond and deep relationship with "La Maga" or "La Serva" or whatever name they gave their wet nurse. It was never a true Christian or family name. Perhaps this made it easier to lose that connection with a person who was not really a part of the family, and made it simpler for everyone concerned, when the time came for her to move on.

A wet nurse was always fed the best food, even if the rest of the family did without. She was providing a very important function to the family, so they made sure she had plenty of free vegetables, dairy products, fresh fruit, and plenty of good beer. They said the hops and grains and molasses in the beer increased the milk flow. A good wet nurse could sustain her own child as well as one, and sometimes two, of the children of the "Patrone."

A manner of this practice sometimes took place at our ranch. If a weak or old cow had died during calving, her calf would be taken home and placed in a warm spot in a back room of the house filled with clean straw. Usually there would be a cow or two who had "come fresh." We would take a flannel sheet or worn out garment and rub the mother all over and even down into the teats area so it would be permeated with all the odors that belonged to her. We would wrap the orphan up in the rags making it possible for them to approach the unsuspecting new mother to nurse. She could smell only her own odors, and not those of the calf's real mother. This practice went on two or three times a day and it wasn't long before the new mother had twins. Everybody was happy!

Since we had one of the smaller ranches, and an isolated one, we had no veterinarian available. It was war time and the veterinarians were typically somewhere helping in hospitals or overseas in the field. There was, however, one veterinarian for the county that covered many large ranches. Usually however, if anything went wrong with the herd during the year, we had to take care of it ourselves.

Not only were there no animal doctors, but the usual supply of young cowboys was also gone. There was no one left who could catch a horse, ride it, or do the roping necessary to control a herd. At Montecito, we walked after the herd or rode the old pickup truck. Thank goodness the ranch was on a stretch of fairly level land cut only by a few deep arroyos that carried the flood waters from the rains.

We were able to reach almost every part of the ranch with the truck. Occasionally, we would break one of the truck's springs or puncture a tire. In that case, we would have to walk back to the house to call a friend or neighbor, or someone in town at a filling station, and they would show up hours later with the necessary equipment.

It was about this time that a retired rancher came up with the idea of an iron chute that could be loaded on the back of a pickup truck. They consisted of large, squared, welded frames with attachments and pulleys. They were built on rollers and could be pushed off the bed of the truck quite easily and rolled to the head-gate of the corral. Each animal could be coaxed into it where a heavy steel rod that curved over the neck secured the animal. With some adjustments, the animal's legs were suspended and it could not walk away or fight the constraints. So, with a proper pulley, the animal could be put on its side or back and any and all necessary work could be done – from branding, vaccinating, castrating, sewing up cuts, or de-horning.

During the almost four years that Dad and I drove back and forth from Cimarron to Montecito Ranch, we had developed a herd of almost 150 head. We had both lost weight and we were always tired. We had to do everything from fighting prairie fires to fixing flat tires – even with loads of hay, grain or water on the truck. Our feet and backs were constantly giving us trouble.

There are two chapters of the Montecito story that stand out in my mind above all others. One was the soul-wrenching story of Star, one of our best thoroughbred white-faced cows. That part of New Mexico sometimes has its worst wind and snow storms in the spring. If a new calf was born during the night, it had to be protected from the freezing weather so we tried to keep the mothers with "show" near the corrals. However, range cattle have a habit of wandering off to hide in an arroyo or cleft in the hills to have their calf.

In early May, we noticed that Star was "near her time." We had been watching her closely just as we did all the others that would be calving. One day we noticed that she had disappeared. We knew she must be up in the hills somewhere, possibly miles from home. We packed up our lunch and water bottle and a rope, and left the ranch house and corrals to start the search. It took us almost three hours of criss-crossing the uneven country and going up and down and across the arroyos; most of the time on foot. Finally, we found her. When she heard us call, she looked up from the deep dry wash she was in as if to say, "It took you long enough!"

We knew at a glance that she was in trouble. We put on our gloves and picked up the rope and walked down into the arroyo with some difficulty. Apparently, she had been trying to have the calf for a day or two. On close examination, we noticed that the calf's head was pulled back into the womb, and the little sharp point of the chest was all that was protruding. We new this happened occasionally, and a trained, strong-armed veterinarian could push the calf back into the birthing canal and twist the head into proper birthing position.

Star knew we were trying to help. She did not fight or move. She only groaned, and saliva flowed from her mouth in long stretching streams. Her eyes were filling with dust and dry particles, and the flies had gathered up into her nose. Dad and I knew there was no possible chance to get to that one veterinarian in Raton in time. Besides, he was probably out on the range helping at the big ranches, like the WS or CS.

We finally coaxed Star to a level area in the gulch where we could drive the truck to. By this time, Star had lain on her side in the sandy bottom, and we attached a rope to the calf. We weren't sure whether we had looped the rope around the calf's neck, or front leg, or even ears. We tied the other end to the truck, eased the vehicle into gear, and gradually began to pull. We pulled slowly, trying to remove that baby from the birthing canal, but it was stuck so firmly that we finally realized we were dragging that poor, suffering creature to her death.

We normally carried a gun in the car, but to our horror we found we had left it in Cimarron that morning. We untied Star and her baby and, as it was now getting dark we had to find our way back to the ranch house slowly and carefully. The old couple at the ranch house didn't own a gun, so we drove home in the dark to Cimarron and did not speak to one another the whole way.

Mom knew something had happened when she saw us step off the truck and into the kitchen. We were drawn and tired and my clothes were covered with mud and blood. She didn't ask the usual questions, but waited until we had bathed and put on fresh clothes and quietly put the food on the table.

The next morning the sun had just started to show on the horizon when Dad and I checked the gun for bullets. We picked up a shovel in the garage. Mom had a lunch packed. Then we left, stopping only long enough for gasoline. On the way to Montecito, Dad made a point of not talking about Star, and I was thankful for that. He talked about Italy and about Egypt where he had worked on the first Aswan Dam at the age of eighteen to make enough money to go to America and this beautiful land of promise. At Montecito we didn't take the time to feed the animals but drove directly to the distant arroyo in the hills.

Star heard us coming and she lifted her head to stare at us and her tail moved up and down in the dust. It was her eyes that hurt me so. They seemed to be begging through the flies and the dirt, "Please do something." I didn't stay around to watch Star's final chapter, but wandered off up the arroyo. Still, I jumped when the crack of Dad's rifle split the morning air. In the years since, I've seen that same imploring look in the eyes of patients in hospitals, and especially in nursing homes. Perhaps someday we will learn to read that unspoken language that comes only from the heart and soul.

We were in the process of repairing fence and corrals at Montecito Ranch and had stopped in Springer to get long, slender cedar posts. We bought steeple nails and borrowed a wire stretcher from the man at the hardware store. I always liked the odor of cedar posts, but it was always a good idea to wear good, strong, leather gloves because handling the rough bark caused the flesh to pucker and break out.

That time of the year the ground had enough dampness in it to make it easy to dig the post holes, and then again the odor of formant, decaying earth filled the mind with visions of onions and garlic "sets" that you place in the garden in Spring.

Wild rabbits would hop away from us and stop short to watch the strange creatures who were down on their knees working on the ground. The sound of the pounding of the steeple that attached the barbed wire to the hard cedar posts would startle them, but their curiosity got the best of them and they would stop again to watch and listen. In the course of a morning we would pick out two of the young, fat rabbits and kill them with the .22 rifle so that we could fry them with garlic and parsley for dinner. They tasted just like young chicken fryers.

During the drives back and forth to the Ranch, Dad and I would have long conversations about the War. My brother, Bill, was in Italy in the Monte Cassino area, fighting with the U.S. Army when they were trying to storm that fortress. My father had been there and in his mind's eye he could envision the battle and the dead bodies that would come home in bags, or remain buried there in some forest. My father was bitter in those days to think that he had left Italy and come to America to find a better life for his sons, only to end up sending them back to Europe, in their prime, to die in the country he had left.

My husband was in the Pacific arena. He had been taking part in one landing after another in those stinking, marshy Japanese-infiltrated places. Each time he came through safely from one of those landings, we would rejoice and be thankful, but in the bottom of our hearts we knew that every bullet out there had a number, and sooner or later, if you kept exposing yourself, that bullet would have your number on it. Many of our discussions concerned president Roosevelt. Dad didn't like the idea of "Unconditional Surrender" because that would lengthen the war, and sooner or later the star in our window, as in other homes, could easily turn from blue to gold – signifying a military death in the family.

We turned out the front gate that led to the highway home, we were tired and hungry, but we both felt a good feeling of accomplishment. The fence would be in good shape for another year, and we wouldn't have a stray calf come in from the neighbor's herd and our cattle would stay in their own pasture.

Mom met us at the door when we arrived home. "Did you hear on the radio that President Roosevelt is dead?"

Dad put out the fire smoldering on the end of his narrow, strong Tuscano Italian cigar on the edge of the car door. His only comment was, "Damn it to hell." I threw off the scarf tied around my long hair. I walked into my bedroom, pulled off my boots and fell sobbing onto the pillow of my bed.

Thank God For the Lovely Burro in My Life

I never saw a real cow pony or horse until I was a grown woman. In my part of the country it was a creature called the burro that was the beast of burden as well as the king of transportation and the growing community of Cimarron, New Mexico. Even the school boys would ride one from Old Town to the school grounds just across the street from my house.

I, too, was delighted with the occasional free rides that I would get on someone's burro. My skirts would fly in the breeze and the bows tied into my long braids would bounce on the back of the burro like butterflies. One of the nice parts about these shaggy beasts was that it was a safe kind of play for both the children and the burro. Rarely was anyone stepped on or kicked, or fell from any great height since the animals were so short, slow, and lazy. They moved so slow that, from a distance, a loaded burro sometimes seemed like a slow-moving part of the landscape.

The nice thing about a burro is that you don't need a saddle to ride one. A short piece of rope and a stick could maneuver you anywhere you wanted to go. They were short, stocky animals. Children could climb all over them and slide off easily. The burro preferred to stand still and would only move when pulled by a rope or slapped by a stick. They ate practically anything from wild grasses to tree limbs and leaves. Apples and carrots, or even an old cabbage, was considered a treat by these animals. If they finally decided to give the children a treat with a little bucking, it came in the form of short hops in one spot and maybe a bray or two. The children hopped around on their backs and squealed with delight.

In the modern jet-age, when it is not unusual for a family to own and operate several cars, it is interesting to note that the burro has not been entirely eliminated. In these days when one of the major problems of colleges and universities is finding student parking for all the vehicles, it may seem strange that the historic burden-bearer, the burro, is still holding his own in certain areas of the West.

There are still approximately 200 burros, or "pack-jacks" as they are called, at the Philmont Boy Scout Ranch four miles to the south of Cimarron. The burro herd at the Philmont is the largest maintained for a specific purpose in the United States, if not in North America, and are the remainder of a herd that at one time numbered nearly 500. The headquarters of the nationally known scout ranch is on land that lies along the eastern base of the snow-capped

Sangre de Cristo Range of northern New Mexico and southern Colorado. It was a unique, but good fortune to have so many of these great and colorful creatures in that part of New Mexico that ended up playing such an important part of boy scout training.

Little did I know as a child where that animal had come from historically, and how many households of furniture, beds, blankets, and tipi poles it had carried across the plains and over the mountains in its time. The burro is closely tied to the history of the Southwest, including north-western New Mexico and parts of Colorado.

In ancient times the Pueblo Indians crossed the Sangre de Cristos to hunt buffalo and antelope in the Apache-Comanche plains country east of the mountains. The route they used was called the Taos Trail, and it crossed the present-day Philmont by way of Agua Fria Creek, Rayado Lodge, Bonita Valley, and Crater Lake. At a later date, the mountain men and frontier scouts used this trail, and even today one may see large blazes on some of the trees that marked its route. One branch of the Santa Fe Trail entered New Mexico by the way of Uncle Dick Wooten's Raton Pass, passed through Cimarron, Rayado, and crossed what is now the Philmont Scout ranch, and went on to Fort Union and Santa Fe. Today the ruts cut by wagons on the trail can be found in the foothills below the Tooth of Time Peak, not far from the Scout Ranch headquarters.

The Philmont Scout Ranch, comprising of 137,221 acres of rugged mountains and plains country, ranges in altitude from 6,500 to 12,441 feet. The burros there play a very important part in the hiking and camping program of the Scout Ranch. The burro, the historic burden-bearer for man, has virtually disappeared from the Southwest, an expansive domain within which he began cutting trails with his hard hoofs more than three and one-half centuries ago. The burro accompanied the Spanish conquistadors into New Mexico and from that region his trails spread across mountains and desert terrain. The long-eared one has been explorer, prospector, miner, rancher, transporter of all goods, and companion to mankind. His labors were indispensable to the development of the West and so he became an institution.

The story of the pack-jacks provides a theme that can be inter-woven into the history of this part of the West, a story that begins with the Spanish Conquistadors, and includes the buffalo hunters, and the mountain scouts and trailblazers. Burros were probably introduced into the region by Alvar Nunez Cabeza de Vaca in the 1530's. He and his three companions wandered for eight years throughout the vast wilderness north of the Gulf of Mexico. They were the first white men to explore this section of America. His stories of this part of the West became the basis of the old Spanish folktale of the "Seven Cities of Cibola."

In 1598, Juan Oñate was sent from Mexico to Santa Fe and Taos to establish the first permanent Spanish settlements in the western foothills of the Sangre de Cristos (Blood of Christ) Mountains. Later, it was the American frontiersman and pioneers who, ever restless, pushed westward. These adventurous pioneers crossed the Alleghenies and settled into the rich, free farmland east of the Mississippi and Missouri rivers. From these farmlands sprang a new crop of western adventurers who conquered the plains and mountains of the West and Southwest. These frontiersmen fought and pushed the Indian before them and finally faced the Spanish who claimed the land between the great central rivers and the Rocky Mountains.

Soon the Spanish realized they were outnumbered by these hardy frontiersmen and that this great region—chiefly the Louisiana Territory—was slipping from their grasp and they knew they must act swiftly. They sold the territory to Napoleon de France, who resold it to the United States in 1803. For fifteen million dollars the young American nation gained a new empire, and a foothold on its destiny as a continental power.

However, it was the Mountain Men and others who first developed the area of the West that is now part of the Philmont Scout Ranch, and men such as Kit Carson, Charles Bent, Lucien B. Maxwell, Don Jesus Abreu, Carlos Beaubien, and Guadalupe Miranda left their mark in this part of the country. But the burro was here before them and he is still a part of the Southwest.

The Philmont Boy Scout Ranch was once a part of the famous Maxwell Land Grant. Lucien B. Maxwell owned the largest ranch in the Old West. For the sum of $2745, Lucien B. Maxwell had taken the first step in a destiny that finally saw him become the largest individual landowner in the history of the United States.

By 1865, Lucien Maxwell had become one of the most prominent men in northern New Mexico. He had built on the Cimarron River a many-roomed mansion complete with servants, hardwood floors and silver service—a suitable place for his life as a feudal baron. One hundred thousand sheep grazed his range, and his cattle and horses increased prodigiously. His "bank," the bottom drawer of an old dilapidated pine bureau, sagged with currency. Maxwell's ranch, with its three story gristmill, corrals, stables, and manor house, became the hub of the Cimarron country. Wayfarers of every sort had standing invitations to dine and rest as Maxwell's guests, and it was not unusual for thirty men to be seated at his table.

Thus, well over a century ago, in 1858, a single individual began the process by which the Maxwell Land Grant was finally consolidated under single ownership—1,714,764 acres or 2,680 square miles, a holding which has understandably stirred the imagination of Americans ever since.

Is it any wonder that the burro played such an important part in this section of the country? Little did this immigrant girl of Italian parents know at the time that she was in the middle of, and played an important part in, Western history.

I Always Knew She Was Etruscan

It was after I read D.H. Lawrence's Etruscan Places that I realized that at least a part of my Italian background stemmed from the Etruscan culture. Although my parents had not mentioned this fact to me as a child, I was determined to find out for myself if there was any connection. The years went by and finally I had the opportunity to take several courses at the University of Colorado concerning Etruscan culture and art. The more I studied and read on the subject, the more I seemed to find my Mother, Divina, in those pages. Many of the beliefs and superstitions I had noted in her philosophy of life and the way she raised her children were straight out of Etruscan life. My mother was a beautiful woman and, from what my father told me, a fine ballroom dancer. She was very popular and although she spoke only limited English, she spoke well with her beautiful dancing eyes and the toss of her blonde hair stacked up on top of her head.

My Father was completely different. He was relaxed, laughed and sang a lot, and his ideas were full of hope. He was adaptable and welcomed change. That is why he could fit so easily into the American way of life here in his new country.

My Mother, on the other hand, did not like change. Many of her decisions had to do with the dreams she had almost every night. She liked to talk about them with the family over the breakfast table. Not many were concerned with happy things. Most of them foretold evil or pain or death. She always mentioned muddy water or spilled blood. Even in her wakeful moments during the day when I was out with her in the garden in the Spring, spading up the fragrant earth and spreading the chicken manure before turning it under, she would stop and lean on her shovel and look around at the distant hills or the weather. If she happened to spot a flight of birds, she would drop her shovel and push back the scarf from her forehead and follow them with her eyes until they were lost over the horizon.

"Eh, Nita," she would say, "the weather is going to change drastically," or "we are in for several weeks of Winter."

Whenever someone butchered a hog, she always wanted to make sure they would save the liver and heart in a bucket she would keep ready for them. As a child, I always thought she was anxious to bake it, surrounded by basil, onions, garlic, and parsley and stab it full of rosemary. But later I found that before she wrapped the liver in the film of membrane that surrounds it, she would spread it out on the large wooden bread board and look at it very intensely. I thought she was looking for impurities or even worms. She never explained but would nod her head and murmur under her breath and later place it in the Dutch oven and slide it into the oven of the coal and wood stove that had been warming up for several hours.

Weeks or months after having divined a liver, when a letter would reach us from Italy, my Mother would say "Ecco, I knew it! My aunt, the one from Aulla, died from a bad chest congestion." We never asked her how she happened to know it, but if she were alive today, she'd say that she received an omen from the liver months before. Later in my research, I learned that the Etruscans studied the livers and hearts of many animals, especially those of the wild boars of the region, which hunters had acquired in the forest nearby.

By the time I was involved in my studies at the university, my children were grown and out on their own. Even though my husband, Curt, was finding it more and more difficult to walk and maneuver about, I found that I could stand it no longer. The time had come for me to see my homeland for the first time. I needed to visit the Old Country and the home of the Etruscans. I met with his doctor who had taken care of him since the first signs of his Parkinsonian condition. I asked the doctor if he thought the two of us could go on an extended trip to Italy. He said he could see no reason why not, especially since Curt was now established on his medication, El Dopa. The El Dopa controlled the shaking and stumbling and even helped with the speech impediment. As long as Curt took the medication at special times and ate a well-rounded diet and had plenty of exercise and walking every day, we should have no difficulty traveling to Italy.

Curt was not too excited about taking the trip. He kept saying "What do we have over there?" He preferred leading the quiet, daily routine at home now that he had retired from his lectures at the University. He enjoyed his meals on time and the trips up to the Ranch to fish in the late afternoons and his weekly game of poker with his retired friends here at the house.

At this time, he was also working on a political novel that he had started several years earlier. He had run for the U.S. Senate in Colorado and had taught Political Science so he was knowledgeable about the trials, pitfalls, and burdens involved with the family, and the bank account, when running for national office. He did not win that election, but he gained a lot of insights into Political Science that he had not learned at Harvard where he received his Ph.D..

As I think back to this stage in my life, I am amazed how determined I was to go to Italy. I realized that this might be the last time we could take this kind of venture together in a foreign land, living under foreign conditions. The part that gave me courage to go to Italy was the opportunity to study Etruscan culture and art that I had read about. The fact that I spoke the Italian language made it all the more practical and exciting.

I made all the arrangements for our trip to Italy—the passports, airline reservations and so forth. By this time, Curt's disease had caused him to become more submissive and dependent. Often, he followed me around, much like a child. As long as he had his three meals a day and a comfortable place to nap, he seemed happy and, thank goodness, he never complained of any pain.

The trip was my first to Europe, and I have to admit, I was scared. Having the responsibility of a semi-invalid wouldn't make it any easier. At this stage, Curt could easily fall and I had to help him maneuver stairways or uneven streets and watch for doors, elevators, and people walking towards him. All it would take was one bad fall to cause the end of the adventure for both of us. A broken hip or arm would make us return to our home in the Rocky Mountains, probably never to venture out again.

Although my family had some distant relatives in the region we were going to visit, we had totally lost contact with them over the years and across the miles. I remembered some of the names of the small towns that my parents had told me about—names like Prota, Tarquinia, Cerveteri, Ostia, and Corte Vecchia. Apparently, my parents had never ventured to Rome or Florence or Genoa or Milan. The largest city they ever mentioned was Specia, a large seaport at the northern end of Italy.

When we arrived in Italy, we decided to live in a third floor apartment in Ostia on the shore of the Mediterranean. Ostia is an old Etruscan city, and the excavations and restorations were not far from where we lived. It was a good location because we could take the train to Rome for the day if we wished, or drive to nearby cities that were once thriving Etruscan cities like Tarquinia, Corte Vecchia, and others.

We would pack some cheese, fruit, boiled chestnuts, and a bottle of wine and drive, for instance, to Cerveteri. We would walk around the small town and ask how to find "the cities of the dead." Generally, they would be a few miles out of the new city, across a meadow and small forest and generally between two old stream beds. The restoration was well done and you could walk down the rows of round-topped mounds of bedrock into which the rooms had been carved out for housing the individual families of the dead.

Usually, very few people were about and we could follow the stone walks right into the vaulted rooms. In the semi-darkness we could see the ledges where the sarcophagi had been placed which were now gone, and on the walls were the pegs where personal belongings of the dead had once hung. There was no doubt that someone had been here before us. Some of the artifacts had been stolen by grave robbers, others had been moved by archaeologists and the government to be placed in special museums.

We walked until Curt could no longer go much farther, and we ended up at the buildings that made up the museums. At the door we were usually greeted by two Italians in uniform who would collect a small amount of money which would give us the opportunity to walk through the rooms cluttered with dusty vases and terra cotta figures.

When the attendants found that I spoke Italian, they were very interested in knowing why I had come from across the world to see this part of Italy. I told them my parents had gone to America when they were young to seek a new life, and had left their families and all their background behind them.

They shook their heads and asked "Eh como anno trava-to la America?" (And how did they find America?)

I told them about my Father's experience in the coal mines in New Mexico, including the strikes and hardships, and later his life-saving talent of muratore (stone masonry) and how my parents settled in a small western town and raised a family there. They were interested to know that Narciso built an Opera House there only to find out that nobody was interested in opera. They laughed when I told them that he quickly converted the Opera House into a silent movie palace and dance hall. "Mi guarda," they murmured.

They wanted to know how many children were born of this union between Narciso and Divina. I told them there were four, two sons and two daughters. The two sons attended law schools and became lawyers and judges; the two daughters tried to find good husbands and were certainly lucky at that. My sister married a man in a thriving business, and I ended up married to a college professor. They kept nodding their heads saying, "Guarda, chi miraculo!" (what a miracle!).

I looked at the two men standing in the open doorway leading into the world that once existed over two thousand years ago. Both of these men were the ages of my brothers, and they spent their days in this ancient valley. Invaders destroyed the Etruscan culture and mysteries, and the language had been lost in a struggle to survive. The males had been killed and the women had been carried away and much of their beautiful art had been destroyed. The round rock houses that had clung to the hillsides leading down to the rivers and oceans were abandoned.

Suddenly, I knew why I had come here. My husband, the Professor of Political Science, had no idea what a fulfillment this was for me. The two Italians here in their boring outpost on this Etruscan hillside had no idea what had happened to this middle-aged woman from Colorado, U.S.A. There was no way and not enough time to try to explain it.

As the evening sun began to drop slowly behind the distant hills, we decided we should have something to eat in one of the little local restaurants we had noticed before beginning our drive back to our apartment in Ostia. I noticed a little yellow card at the door of one establishment that said they were serving Polenta e Stufado de Coniglio (cornbread and rabbit stew).

My heart actually fluttered with excitement. My mother had raised me on polenta and stews made of rabbit, or venison, or pheasant, or whatever my father had killed during the hunt in the vast, wide-open expanses of the New World.

We walked into the warm, fragrant dining room. A gentleman with a towel draped over his arm met us and directed us to a small table for two with a low burning candle on it. I immediately spoke to him in Italian and ignored the menu he handed me. I told him how happy I was that the specialty of the house that night was Polenta e Stufado de Coniglio. His eyes brightened and a beautiful wide Italian smile crossed his face and he remarked that he didn't expect to hear Italian coming from such an obviously American couple.

The kindness, the attention, and the wonderful food with the background of an old man playing an accordion and singing, "O Solo Mio" made the evening complete and memorable for me. My father had sung that song to me through all the years when I was growing up in that Opera House turned into an American silent movie house a long, long way from here.

Just above our heads on the wall were two portraits and two flags. One was a portrait of the Pope and the other of John F. Kennedy. Between them were draped two flags. One was Italian and the other the beautiful American Stars and Stripes.

My salty tears mingled with the sauce in the rabbit stew. I'll never have a more wonderful meal or moment in my life.

Suddenly I was homesick.

The Legend of the
Three Glass Beads

This story is the result of a very interesting discovery that my son, whose name is also Curtis Martin, like his father's, made during an archaeological investigation in west central Colorado recently. That part of the country is becoming one of the rich wine-growing and producing areas in the United States and that means the planting of grapes. Some of the vineyards are experimental stations, planted on public lands. As a result, professional archaeologists are hired to walk over the area before the clearing of growth and the leveling of the land for the miles of grape vines that will soon cover it, to insure that no ancient Indian campsites or burial grounds will be disturbed.

It was during one of these archaeological investigations that Curtis found the three glass beads of this story, on the floor of an old, but still standing, set of wooden tipi poles.

The site was the location of a Ute Indian encampment at some time in the late Nineteenth Century.

When Curtis told me about the find, those early historic beads and I seemed worlds apart. What is the magic and the circumstances that brought my son, and through him myself, together with these artifacts from over 100 years ago? Perhaps my son, as part of his job, will study these tiny glass gems through powerful microscopes, photograph and sketch them, measure the diameter of each, and write about their historic meaning and importance. He tells me that these three beads—bright blue, white, and brick-red "seed beads"—were crafted far away from where they were found, and a couple of cultures away. He tells me that they were hand blown in glass factories on the tiny Island of Murano in the lagoon near Venice, Italy, and then shipped to America for trade to the Native Americans.

When I heard this, my personal connection to these relics began to make itself known. For my part, that historic, almost unbelievable connection began in another little Italian village named Prota, in the province of Massa Carrara. A young man was born long ago in Prota, several days travel, in his day, from that glass factory where the beads were made, but in the same time in history. This young man's name was Narciso Federici. My father. He and the love of his life, Divina Mazzoni, my mother, were growing up together in this little mountain town, among the hills and grapes of northern Italy.

Little did they know at the time what the future held for them in a place named America! A place on the other side of the world, where a strange word was spoken, and even the clothes they wore and the food they ate were worlds apart. But destiny plays strange tricks on some of the creatures of this world and I am a direct result of one of destiny's twists of fate. My parents came from a world so different from the one in which I was born, and the one in which I raised my sons, as did those tiny glass beads that Curtis found in that sheltered spot, on the old Indian site near the grape-growing community of Palisade, Colorado.

My story all began as the dream of the young Narciso Federici. He wanted something more, something different, something better for himself and his future children than what he saw for himself if he stayed on in Prota, Italy. Little did he know that the morning he walked to the nearby town of Aulla to buy tobacco and salt that his destiny was going to start down the long road to America. Little did he know that his destiny was going to parallel that of three little glass beads that were being formed from molten glass at the same time on the other side of northern Italy.

When Narciso walked into the small market he noticed some well-dressed Englishmen talking to the shop owner in broken Italian. The Englishmen were looking for expert Italian stonemasons; men that could cut stone well enough to build a dam across the River Nile in Egypt, many miles from that part of the world. In those days, before dams were created by huge, monstrous machines that dropped endless supplies of cement from their mouths, what was needed to contain the waters of a mighty river like the Nile were thousands of massive blocks of precisely-cut stone.

That is why the Englishmen had come to Massa Carrara. It was here that men grew up cutting the beautiful marble of the local mountain into huge flawless blocks. Marble that had become world famous. Marble that had been quarried for centuries to build the monuments and temples of the ancient Romans, and the statues of Michelangelo. The dam across the Nile in Egypt needed stone blocks as well; not of marble yet cut so precise that they could be fit together to contain the beautiful staff of life flowing down the river channel, necessary to make the Egyptian desert bloom and flourish.

When the Englishmen in Aulla that fateful morning told my father what they were seeking, and why, it opened up a beautiful vista onto what he had been dreaming of. This opportunity in Egypt would be the first stepping stone in the answer to his prayer that would eventually carry him and his loved one, Divina, away from the poverty and hardships of Prota to America; a world that he had heard was a land of freedom and opportunity, where gold was scattered on the streets.

The story of Narciso and Divina's journey to the wild west of America, where I was born, is a long one, filled with suffering, hard labor and disappointments, yet also one of compassion, love, and the oneness of the world. They were surrounded by strange ways, strange sounds, hunger, cold, heat, mistrust, and discrimination, but also strong family ties and camaraderie between peoples from vastly different backgrounds and cultures. In this new land they learned about the scarcity of water, the rattlesnakes that could kill you or your child with one swift strike, and the coyotes that howled and yelled throughout the night like lost, hungry souls.

The money that my father earned working on the Aswan Dam was used to carry himself and my mother to a huge, open, empty land; New Mexico. There were no fields full of grapevines and no chestnut trees here, like there were back home. Where were the quiet, colorful homes with open doors and laughing children? Where were the horse-drawn carts filled with food—the cheeses, the breads, the fruits and vegetables from the gardens—the sounds of singing the old songs like O'Solo Mio, and the large casks of fragrant wine? And where were the golden nuggets what were supposed to be littering the streets? What happened to the dream?

With time, and patience, Narciso and Divina found work in the coal mines and cattle ranches of New Mexico, and eventually my father discovered that his future lay in his ability to cut stone; the talent learned in the mountains of Massa Carrara as a young man, and later in the deserts of Africa on the River Nile. The homes and stores that he was hired to build in his new hometown of Cimarron have changed hands many times, but they still stand snug, strong, and sound.

Five children were born to the new American couple—I was the second. Only four of us survived to adulthood, to attend schools, start careers, raise families, and become worthwhile citizens. From the four of us new generations of children, grandchildren, and great-grandchildren sprung; now teachers, lawyers, merchants, doctors, parents, writers, and poets, among them an archaeologist, my son, Curtis.

At the same time that Narciso and Divina were making their way across the Atlantic Ocean to Ellis Island on the eastern shores of America, and from there by train across the broad plains, mountains, and deserts to the wilds of New Mexico, three glass beads—one blue, one white, and one brick-red—had also found their way from Italy to New York and from there into the hands of a trader who had carried them west along with thousands of similar beads and numerous other stores and trinkets to trade to the Indians; precious metal knives and axes, guns and bullets, pots and pans, mirrors and baubles and magic things of all kinds.

The three tiny glass beads, no bigger than the head of a pin, found their way to the moccasin of a young Ute woman in western Colorado just as a young emigrant couple from the same homeland found their way to northern New Mexico. Once here, despite all of the differences of language and culture, that couple discovered how truly alike all of mankind is. When it came down to people in need, one discovers that we all have the same ten fingers, and the same beating heart. Perhaps it is simply curiosity, such as that of a young Italian stonemason seeking a better future, or that of an archaeologist seeking insights into the past, that can lead us to all that we need to know in this day and age.

Perhaps those three glass beads somehow are a symbol of what the modern world needs so desperately to survive and move on; the knowledge that all of the peoples of the world are, after all, simply members of the same Human race, all living on the same small, blue planet spinning through space. Maybe the story of the three beads teaches us that we are all of the same cloth; mortal beings with a heart that pumps life's strength through our bodies; souls with the same needs for shelter, sustenance, respect, and love. Why does it seem so difficult in these times for some peoples and cultures to allow those simple needs to others, and, in fact, to all living creatures?

The Making of a Sculptor (after 60)

It wasn't until I had spent considerable time in Italy in 1972 that I decided that when I returned to Boulder I would do two things: study the Italian language, culture, and art, and try to find some kind person or persons that would teach me the fundamentals of sculpture.

The road to this decision was long and crossed many paths but perhaps if I give you just a glimpse of how some people finally come to a decision like this, you will find that perhaps a similar thing has happened in your lifetime. Or, perhaps, you may know a friend or a parent that might decide that it's not too late to make a drastic decision and start from scratch on a new direction– no matter how old they happen to be.

I was born of immigrant parents who came to America because they heard it was the land of promise. They settled in New Mexico – mostly because my father could pick up a piece of land there in an area known as Apache Hill under the Homestead Act.

He found it was impossible to make a living farming or ranching at Apache Hill so my father, having learned the trade of stone masonry in his native land and in Egypt, soon started constructing most of the stone homes and business establishments in the small town of Cimarron. He soon had a good reputation and although they couldn't pronounce his name, Narciso Federici, they soon adopted his nickname of "Fred Narciso." He built the Opera House, the church, the school, the hotel, the bars, the one and only general store and many of the homes of the wealthy Englishmen that had come to mine and ranch in that area. I was born in the living quarters on the first floor of the Opera House. Besides building structures, my father also cut many headstones of coral limestone for the cemetery on the hill outside of town, which can be found there today.

Before I attended the local public school, I could only speak Italian and Spanish, the languages I learned at home and among my little friends. I learned English for the first time at school and also taught my mother and father how to speak and read English by using the schoolbooks and tablets that I brought home. I was nine to thirteen years of age then. I attended a one-room schoolhouse at a place named Colfax, New Mexico and later at Dawson, a coal-mining town. They are now both ghost-towns.

I married my husband, Curtis Martin, at the age of eighteen in Taos, New Mexico. He was teaching at that time in a one-room schoolhouse in Trinchera, Colorado. Then World War II engulfed us and we were separated for three years. During that time I returned to Cimarron to live with my parents while we ran cattle on the ranch out in the plains near Springer. After the war Curtis attended Harvard University where he received his PhD before we returned to the West. He took a job as a professor of Political Science at the University of Colorado in Boulder where we built our first home and raised two sons, Brooke and Curt.

Quite suddenly, it was 1972, the boys were gone to their respective schools, and that is when we decided to take off for an extended stay in Italy to find my roots. It was at this time that I discovered that my origins had sprung from the Etruscan area of northern Italy. While we were there we lived in Ostia, a seaside town on the Mediterranean. Ostia was once a thriving Etruscan seaport. The original city, Ostia Antiqua, has been excavated and preserved. The local farmers still find three to four thousand year old artifacts and pot shards as they dig in their fields—so much older than the artifacts and pottery fragments I found as a child on our ranch at Apache Hill, New Mexico. My son, Curt, who is now an archeologist, tells me that they are only 900-1000 years old by comparison.

While I was at Ostia I became feverishly interested in Etruscan art and culture. I visited all the libraries and museums, nearby and in Rome, and spent time speaking to the local residents in places like Cerveteri, Tarquinia, and Civita Vechia.

When we returned to Boulder after the trip, at the age of 60, I entered the University to become a student for the first time since the little one-room school in Colfax, New

Mexico. I completed all the classes offered in Italian language, history, and art history. I also took 21 hours of Chicano studies because that too was a part of my background, having grown up in the Hispanic area of New Mexico. I met Professor John Wilson and expressed my interest in sculpture. He speaks Italian and cooks Italian, so we got along very well. He started me off by making me take a lot of introductory classes like sketching, art history, etc. My first classes in sculpture were very boring because I had to work with cardboard, wire, old automobile parts, plastic, etc. Finally, John gave me my first sculpting tool, a mallet. I eventually had to cut off part of the handle because I discovered that made it become as much a part of my hand as possible.

John learned from our long conversations that I was only interested in stone, wood, bronze and ceramics, and he understood my interest in the old Greek and Italian sculpture, so he let me go my own way as did Professors Chamberlain and Wolfe. They were my three mentors. I was soon learning about the different tools and the different kinds of stone and wood and how to fashion and fire the ceramic pieces. The terra cottas that I had seen in Etruscan country influenced my work a great deal. I think all three professors tried their best to get me away from that influence but every time I started a new piece, sooner or later, there would emerge the image of the art of my ancestors.

Many of my pieces made John smile because he has known and studied the work of the Spanish wood carvers of New Mexico and occasionally a piece of mine, especially in wood or stone, would have the influence of the Santeros of New Mexico. I had seen a lot of that kind of art in the homes of my friends there as I grew up. Every home had its crude Santos or Manotables.

All three of my professors showed a continuing interest in my work long after I graduated, and would occasionally come out to encourage me and see what I was working on. Perhaps it was merely my spaghetti and wine, or all of the sweet basil that I raised in profusion in my garden that they liked! Anyway, they had come at the right time in my life when I had gone full circle and finally found myself. All I need now is some peace and time for me.

Now, what are the difficulties involved with a woman my age that wants to sculpt? It is very hard work, especially if you are interested in the medium of stone or wood, or even bronze and terra cotta. It takes a lot of the latest power tools as well as lifting and moving devices and it takes a strong back as well as strong hands and arms. So you can imagine the disadvantages for a woman, especially at my age. Not only that, but the kind of stone that I like to sculpt is very expensive and hard to find.

I remember reading some of the art history of the early sculptors in Italy. They would wait along the roadways for the wagons and carts carrying the large pieces of marble coming down from the Massa Carrara quarries in northern Italy and if a particularly good stone came along, they fought with swords to see who would get it. They say that many of the stones that Michelangelo used were obtained just in that way.

Every piece of stone is different, even if it comes from the same quarry. There is lots of variety in the color, and the natural defects—the soft spots or the cracks in the stone—that all are a part of determining the finished result. Often, an individual stone shows potential for only a single idea in the sculptor's mind, and many times the artist has to make adjustments for breaks, etc. and ends up doing something entirely different from the original idea. Michelangelo said that "the image is in the stone, you have only to let it out." I have found it so.

In Boulder, good stone and wood for sculpting were hard to find and cost a great deal. In wood as well as stone, there are properties that make for the best sculpture. The hard woods are difficult to find and some of my pieces came from Arizona, Oklahoma, and even foreign countries. Hard wood gives the best finish and doesn't splinter and break like pine, spruce, and cottonwood.

If you work in bronze you have to depend on a good foundry for the final castings. They too are hard to find and often they don't have all the help they would like and you are put on a waiting list for casting. It sometimes takes 6 months or longer to get a finished piece and it is very expensive. A small head, for instance can cost up to $500 or more and that is without the patina or the back.

Sculpture is hard to ship to galleries and shows around the country. It has to be well packed and heavily insured. Some male sculptors are fortunate in that they have a truck and can often deliver their own. There again the "little old woman in tennis shoes" has a hard row to hoe.

I hate to bring this up, but there is still the idea that women can't sculpt and shouldn't even be considered seriously as sculptors. In some of my classes at CU I was the only woman. Very few of the sculptures in Italy, old or new, are by women. Men liked to sculpt figures of women and children, but "motherhood" was traditionally hailed as one of the most creative subjects, and in many instances it is still true today. Women are supposed to dabble in oil or watercolors, weaving, or ceramics but that's it.

In my hometown there has never been a woman sculptor and very few men with the exception of the Spanish men who still sculpt the Santos. I think the fact that I was asked to give a one-woman show in Boulder was mostly because of curiosity.

Ceramic sculpture is by far my favorite kind of sculpture. The trouble with ceramic sculpture is that you have to have a good kiln in which to fire it and that presented a problem in those days in Boulder. Terra Cotta is malleable and gives you such a good feeling of the real creation of your object. Your hand and head as well as your heart are involved in sculpture and that brings about your own identity in the sculpture. The Etruscans were past masters at it and suitable clay was plentiful in that part of Northern Italy. They had plenty of marble, as the mountains near them were solid marble, and they also had clay and mines for metal.

One thing the Etruscans didn't have was wax and they had to trade with the ships coming from Asia Minor for wax. For the "lost wax" method you had to have a lot of wax and they also used it, as well as honey, for embalming the dead. Even in the middle-ages sculptors had to go around begging for left over candle wax from the churches, and they used it over and over.

I became interested in the art and culture of the Etruscans the first time I read about them in a book entitled Etruscan Places written in the early 1940s by D.H. Lawrence. If you are interested in the Etruscan culture of Italy and their importance to history and the history of art you should also read a delightful book written by a young Englishman named George Dennis; Cities and Cemeteries of Etruria. He was an English councilman at Civita Vechia in Italy between the years of 1842-1847. The book was published in 1848. It is the most vivid and charming, as well as accurate, book on the subject. I walked all over that area the year I was there and visited most of the "cities of the dead" carved into the tufa (compacted volcanic ash spewed from three great craters which are now lakes).

Some of my relatives walked me out to the hills and meadows in northern Italy. They pointed out the rounded hilltops covered with natural growth—pine and chestnut—and told me that underneath could be found the "cities of the dead Etruscan."

It's strange that my passion for that culture evolved from other hilltops ripe with antiquity clear across the world in New Mexico.

What a small world this has turned out to be for me.

Tears

Generally it came on a Sunday afternoon when all the family and a few old friends had just finished eating some of my mother's excellent cooking. Of course, there had been several bottles of Dad's good old Dago Red along with the ravioli and the big bowl of fresh dandelion greens and home grown swiss chard salad with the olive oil and vinegar dressing that had been mixed well with warm human hands to help the vinegar and oil penetrate the intricate leaves of the greens.

The occasion typically came during a lull in the eating and the chatter of children and the groaning from the aches and pains of the old folks. Dad always seemed to know the right time to take advantage of a captive audience.

My mother could always tell when one of his good stories was coming up and she pretended to try to stop it before it got started, but you could tell she was going to enjoy it too. Hearing her pretend that she was going to be bored by having to sit through the telling of some story by Dad that he had told so many times before, over and over, tickled everyone. They would be convinced that my mother was going to be bored, when the whole time she was playing dad's shadow box, or "straight man", which would actually add a great deal to the telling of the story.

Anyway, one evening he began telling a story that I had heard many times before about a young man in Italy who wanted to come to America. He started out by telling how the young man went around his small town telling everyone that he had finally made all the arrangements to come to America, and even had the local tailor, my uncle Guido, make him a new suit for the trip.

Finally the day came to leave on the adventure and his friends and relatives all joined him at the shipyards to bid him goodbye. They listened as he prayed to his favorite Saint, San Gennaro. The young man promised to buy the saint a new coat if he should make the trip safe and sound to New York and Ellis Island. *"San Gennaro, Benedetto, se mi fai passare sto mare, ti compro lu capoto."*

Sure enough, the story continued, the young man makes the trip in fine shape and the day comes when he goes down the gang plank and upon placing his feet on the natural ground of Ellis Island, he lifts his head and in a good strong Italian voice he says, "Thank you, thank you San Gennaro for helping me come to America. I know I promised to buy you a coat if I made it here safely, but now, come to think of it, go buy your own coat, San Gennaro Benedetto." With that he picks up his old suitcase and heads for the nearest bar!

Everyone had been listening quietly for the punch line as usual, and, as usual, I didn't find it very funny, but everyone else laughed out loud and slapped their knees and beat each other on the back until their faces turned red and the tears came pouring out of their eyes. I guess it was my tender age but I looked and listened all around me and I didn't understand the tears that flowed from all that happiness and thanksgiving. Until now. Now I find that my tears, too, flow in torrents down my cheeks at the thought of that story. If that saint could have helped me cross that ocean, I would gladly have given him my coat.

San Gennaro, Benedetto, se mi fai passare sto mare, ti compro lu capoto. In a way, I feel that I do owe that coat to the patron saint of immigrants. For I have been given the chance to cross that ocean and return to the Old Country; to the land of my ancestors. Not only in person, but also in my heart and soul; through the stories of La Familia that have been passed on to me.

THE END

About the Author

"My story is inextricably woven into the stories of who my parents were, where they came from, what they envisioned for their children, and what they endured to pursue those dreams. The earliest things that I remember about myself and my family occurred at our ranch in Apache Hill, New Mexico. The stories of those eight years provide a unique and meaningful chronicle of an immigrant family that had come to America seeking a new and better life. Now, when I take the time to reflect on those years, I am engulfed with an appreciation of the amount of courage, strength, and patience that it must have taken for my parents to accomplish what they did."

Thus starts Courage of Innocence; the non-fictional account of author Ann Federici-Martin's saga of growing up the daughter of Italian immigrants Narciso Federici and Divina Mazzoni. Her father gathered the strength to leave his family, friends, and impoverished life behind in the hills of northern Italy to follow his dream to L'America where, it was said, "gold grew on trees like apples." But, to get there, Narciso's journey first leads him to Egypt where he worked as a stone mason on the first Aswan Dam to earn his passage across the Atlantic Ocean. His story, and soon thereafter his wife Divina's, pass through the halls of Ellis Island and from there to the frontier of northern New Mexico; land of cowboys, coal miners, cactus, and open range.

Ann's memoirs read like a western novel, set against a backdrop of empty spaces the size of which the immigrants could hardly comprehend. But the family settles into their new, rugged and unpredictable life, and indeed prospers. There were no golden apples, but there were towns and villages of coal miners and cattlemen who needed groceries, homemade "Dago Red" wine, and amusements to offer distraction from their hard lives. The Federici family provided them all. Narciso even built a two-story stone opera house in the village of Cimarron, assuming that these culture-starved Americans would jump at the chance to attend a good Italian opera if it was put before them.